Hamlyn all-colour paperbacks

Frederick Wilki

illustrated by John H. Batchelor
& Arthur Gay

Hamlyn - London
Sun Books - Melbourne

FOREWORD

War has always had a terrible, self-destroying fascination for man. It has probably occupied more time and taken a larger share of effort and wealth than any other of his endeavours. Although war was always a sordid business, time does soften its impact and gives it a false image of glamour and excitement. No period is more prone to be so treated than the Middle Ages with its knights and their gaily bedecked horses. The study of their armour is a fascinating one, although it is but one stage in the long sequence of discoveries and developments that has led from the leather cap of the ancient Middle East right up to the sophisticated, armoured fighting-vehicle of today.

This book shows how the changes in arms and armour have been the result of a constant struggle between the armourer and the weapon-maker. Each improvement in weapon design evoked some response from the armourer, who increased the thickness of plate or added an extra glancing surface. Today the struggle is basically the same, although in place of an armoured knight there is a giant tank and the archer has been superseded by an anti-tank gunner. The once-knightly sword has now become largely an ornament or uniform accessory, and its place has been taken by weapons far more terrible than the early swordsmiths could ever have conceived in their wildest dreams.

F.W.

Published by The Hamlyn Publishing Group Limited
London · New York · Sydney · Toronto
Hamlyn House, Feltham, Middlesex, England
In association with Sun Books Pty Ltd, Melbourne

Copyright © The Hamlyn Publishing Group Limited 1971

ISBN 0 600 00126 1
Phototypeset by Filmtype Services Limited, Scarborough
Colour separations by Schwitter Limited, Zurich
Printed in Holland by Smeets, Weert

CONTENTS

4   Ancient world
12 Classical world
24 Saxons and Vikings
30 Eleventh century
34 Twelfth century
44 Thirteenth century
50 Fourteenth century
60 Fifteenth century
82 Sixteenth century
102 Seventeenth century
120 Eighteenth century
124 Nineteenth century
132 Twentieth century
138 British military swords from 1600
144 Africa
146 America
148 Asia
154 Oddities
156 Glossary
157 Books to read
158 Index

ANCIENT WORLD
Flint

Man's first weapons were almost certainly percussive, the earliest probably being just conveniently shaped branches. However, soon he was also using spears with fire-hardened tips. At what point in time man discovered the cutting properties of flint is not known, but it was the earliest of his major technological discoveries.

Flint is found over wide areas of the earth either on or reasonably close to the surface. The earliest flint implements are known as eoliths, some having a natural cutting edge. Many of those ascribed to early man are disputed by some archaeologists, who claim they are the result of natural formation. But some eoliths are undoubtedly man made, crudely chipped to increase the keenness of the cutting edge.

Man developed his skill and techniques, and two types of flint structures, the flake and the core, were evolved. Flakes were produced by striking the solid flint at an angle, and these sharp, thin pieces could be shaped and used as scrapers, arrowheads, lance-heads, or knives. The thick block or core was also shaped and was most commonly used for the so-called handaxe. The hand-axe and other core tools may have originated in Africa, whereas the flake tools probably came from the East, perhaps China. Skill in shaping enabled early man to produce a few long, thin flakes of flint suitable for use as knife-blades. This technique appears to have originated in the Near East, and such blades were used for wood shaping. No doubt clubs of this period were more sophisticated than the branch of earlier times. Lance-heads were cleverly shaped; some were fashioned with a tang, or shoulder, to make it easier to secure them to the shafts.

With the advent of the Mesolithic period, some twelve thousand years ago, man extended his stone-working skills to other minerals and also began to shape his implements by grinding them. The Neolithic period, about 2500 BC, saw a more general adoption of this technique as well as an overall improvement in the quality of flint implements, which were now polished and smoothed. The use of the bow and arrow, begun in Mesolithic times, now became more widespread.

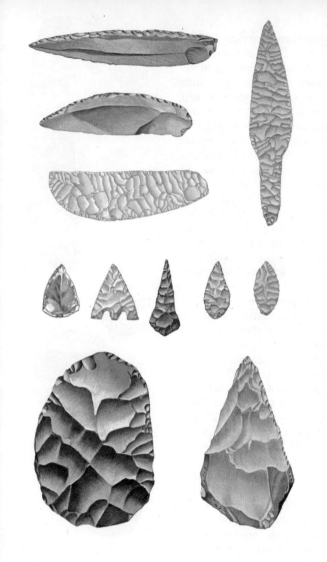

Flint could be fashioned into various tools and weapons. Thin pieces, flakes, could be bound to a haft, long ones serving as lance-heads (*top*) and smaller ones as arrow-heads (*centre*) with or without barbs; larger pieces, cores, made hand-axes (*bottom*).

5

Egyptian warrior

With the urban civilization of Asia Minor the first organized armies were brought into being. Large numbers of men were led into battle as a unit instead of just indulging in a series of individual, haphazard, hand-to-hand combats. Armies included chariots and cavalry in addition to foot soldiers. If the wall paintings of the period are to be accepted at face value, Egyptian troops were all provided with much the same equipment but, in comparison with such countries as Sumer, it was rather primitive.

Although the Sumerian soldier wore a simple form of metal-studded leather cape and a leather or metal helmet, certainly by 2800 BC the Egyptian soldier still had only his shield for defence. Most of the infantry carried a shield which was at first simply an animal skin stretched over a wooden frame. Later it was made rectangular and then given a curved top. Many of the shields were quite small; presumably designed to protect only the head and body. Some circular shields are shown on Egyptian wall paintings, but these were apparently used only by the mercenaries.

Flakes of flint were sometimes fitted to simple handles to form daggers, whilst shaped pieces of rock fitted onto wooden handles made crude but serviceable maces.

6

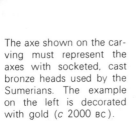

The axe shown on the carving must represent the axes with socketed, cast bronze heads used by the Sumerians. The example on the left is decorated with gold (*c* 2000 BC).

Egyptian weapons

Even when metal came into general use flint and stone were not abandoned completely; they were easily obtainable and continued to be used for the more commonplace weapons. Mace-heads were frequently just a round piece of stone roughly shaped into flanges, with a hole painstakingly drilled through the centre to take a wooden shaft. Flint blades were also fashioned and fitted into hilts which were often carved into attractive shapes and patterns with high relief.

Egyptian stoneworkers utilized other minerals apart from flint, including marble, lapis lazuli, nephrite (a green-coloured stone), obsidian (a black stone), and even amber, although these were primarily for ceremonial rather than practical purposes. Even when metal blades replaced those of stone the minerals were still employed for hilts and for their decorative qualities. Egyptians made considerable use of the bow, both the simple arc form and the double-curved type, and the arrow-heads were still made of flint.

Introduction of metal

Copper was the first metal used by man. This tremendous leap forward was apparently first taken in Anatolia. Its use was known to the Egyptians by the beginning of the fourth millenium, although by then it had been employed elsewhere for a thousand years. Knowledge of this technique spread slowly, probably reaching Europe via Greece and the Balkans. Copper axes and daggers were, however, too soft to hold an edge for very long and therefore needed frequent sharpening.

But copper could be hardened by adding a small amount of tin, and the alloy became known as bronze. Only a small percentage of tin was needed; indeed for daggers and swords only about two per cent was required. Not only was bronze harder, but it was also easier to cast than pure copper.

Iron was first smelted in Asia Minor, and examples of iron objects dating from 3000 BC have been excavated there. The Hittites were the first to work iron in any quantity. It was probably because this fierce race had strong, iron swords that it was able to conquer so much of the known world.

Daggers from Ur and Anatolia (*c* 2500 BC). Axes from Egypt (*c* 2000 BC)

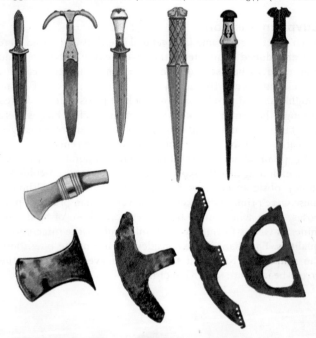

Wooden shields from Egyptian tombs (*c* 2000 BC). Crescent-shaped, cutting-and-slashing swords typical of the sort used by Egyptians and Sumerians (*c* 1900 BC)

Egyptian sword and shield

Egyptian shields were of leather-covered wood, but when metal became more plentiful a boss was added near the top to afford extra strength. Shields for nobles were decorated by adding animal skins, that of Tutankhamen was covered with antelope skin. Tomb paintings show workshops with craftsmen producing these simple shields, and surviving examples are not uncommon. When not in use the shield could be carried on the shoulder by means of a long, leather strap.

Swords were a practical impossibility when only flint was available – they would have been too heavy and fragile. They did not appear until the discovery of metals. Early ones had a straight, tapered blade and were intended essentially as a stabbing weapon. The hilt was secured to the blade by a series of rivets, and the pommel or weight at the top of the grip was often carved into quite attractive shapes. Around 2500 BC the first of the slashing swords was developed and took the form of a carved sickle-shaped blade. This sword, called a *khopesh*, was a popular Egyptian weapon and, indeed, became the symbol of the pharaoh's power. Axes were also popular weapons; the head was lashed to the shaft or fitted on by means of a socket.

9

Light chariots were a feature of Egyptian cavalry. This example, decorated with gold, was buried with its owner in the fifteenth century BC. Chariots often carried an archer, and here a noble holds a double-convex bow and a bunch of reed arrows.

Egyptian chariot

Although the Egyptians were noted for their use of chariots, these came originally from Canaan and appear on stone carvings there as early as 3000 BC. A typical Egyptian chariot was extremely light. By about 1400 BC it had acquired its characteristic form, with two four-spoked wheels, the rims covered with leather, mounted on a single axle which was fixed at the rear of the simple, light body. From the centre of the body projected a shaft some five feet in length, at the end of which was a double yoke to fit over the horses' shoulders, with straps passing round the front of the horses' necks to secure them to the chariot. Many were made as two-man vehicles, holding a charioteer who looked after the horses and an archer or spearman who concentrated on the fighting. Extra arrows or javelins were normally carried in a quiver mounted permanently on the side of the chariot. The body was simply a wooden framework covered with leather or equally lightweight material, and on the royal chariot the sides are shown as being decorated in high relief.

From about 1400 BC the wheel was strengthened; a six-spoked type was adopted and remained more or less standard for all chariots. The horses were frequently richly bedecked, their backs covered with a brightly decorated cloth. Chariots were also used for hunting and conventional transport.

Assyrians

From evidence found on monuments it seems certain that the Assyrian chariot was larger and heavier than that of the Egyptians, and that their armies were far better equipped. Chariot wheels were six spoked with wide, thick rims, and the carriage was large enough to hold three people – a driver, an archer, and a third man whose job seems to have been to guard the others with a round shield. The Assyrians developed larger, more complex vehicles like mobile battering rams. In addition to the chariots there were large bodies of cavalry, archers, spearmen, and slingmen. As well as their main weapon most soldiers also carried a short, straight-bladed sword. Although mail was also used, most wore a protective tunic reaching to the knees or ankles, made of overlapping plates presumably attached to a leather garment.

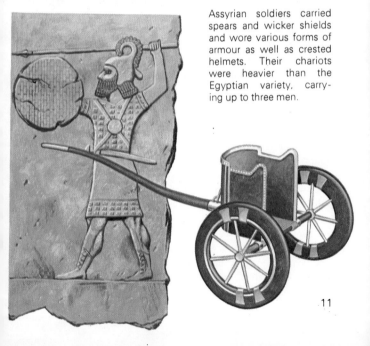

Assyrian soldiers carried spears and wicker shields and wore various forms of armour as well as crested helmets. Their chariots were heavier than the Egyptian variety, carrying up to three men.

CLASSICAL WORLD
Early Greek warrior

Greek armourers and weapon-smiths produced pieces that were not only technically very competent but also aesthetically pleasing. They made great use of bronze for their armour, often employing the springiness of the metal to hold the pieces in position on the body.

Greek tactics were, for centuries, based on the phalanx, a solid formation of spearmen, the hoplites, who advanced to the sound of a pipe and, by their sheer mass, drove back their enemies. There were, of course, many individual combats, and Greek epics abound with accounts of them. The protagonists might well have worn armour or have fought practically naked except for helmet and shield. Mycenaen helmets of around 1500 BC were elaborate, having a leather cap covered with bands of boars' tusks, alternate rows pointing in opposite directions. The large shields were made of leather and wood, with metal reinforcing. Some were like the Egyptians', straight sided with a curved top, whereas others were like a violin in outline.

(*Above*) some hoplites fought nearly naked, but all carried the large, circular shield held by the strap at the rim.

(*Opposite top*) a remarkable set of bronze plate armour dating from the late fifteenth century BC, found at Dendra near Mycenae (*see page 15*).

(*Bottom left*) a reconstruction of a Mycenaen helmet, composed of strips of boar tusk fastened to a leather foundation cap.

(*Bottom right*) Bronze Age swords from Mycenae, intended as slashing weapons. They vary in length from 20 to 30 inches.

Greek equipment

Early Greek swords were fashioned with a straight blade about three feet long and were essentially thrusting weapons. They were made in one piece with a long, narrow bar, the tang, on which was fitted the hilt. Later swords were of the leaf shape so typical of the Bronze Age and had a central, thickened, strengthening rib. The flat, broad blade probably made them suitable for slashing as well as thrusting. Bronze spear-heads with sockets to attach them to the shaft were also cast. Their size suggests that they were thrusting, not missile, weapons.

Greek armour

Perhaps the most characteristic helmet of ancient Greece is that known as the Corinthian. It was first illustrated on vases and bronze figures about 700 BC and was soon widely adopted. It reached down to the shoulder and completely enclosed the head except for a T-shaped opening leaving the nose, eyes, and mouth clear, although a nasal, or projecting bar over the nose, offered further protection here. The entire helmet was hammered out of a single piece of bronze – no mean feat! Surviving examples of the Corinthian have a series of holes around the rim, which clearly indicate that padding and a lining must normally have been fitted. Another common type was that called Illyrian; it was made in two pieces and joined by a ridge running across the crown of the helmet. Its shape was simpler than that of a Corinthian, and the helmet had pointed cheek-pieces.

Less common than the Illyrian and the conventional

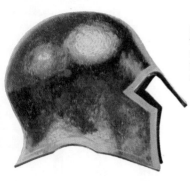

Many hoplites wore the beautifully made and all-enveloping style of helmet usually known as the Corinthian, which appeared as early as 700 BC.

Far simpler to construct was the Illyrian helmet with its pointed cheek-pieces, for it was made in two pieces which were then joined along the top.

A finely embossed helmet from the Mediterranean island of Crete in a style not unlike the mainland Corinthian, except that it had no nose-guard

The Chalcidian bronze helmet was less comprehensive than the Corinthian form, for it had spaces cut for the ears, but was otherwise very similar.

Corinthian helmets was that identified as Chalcidian because it appears on pottery so named by archaeologists. It had open spaces for the ears and a simple nasal. A variation of the Corinthian helmet was produced by the craftsmen of Crete, and this form was smaller in size and decorated with high-relief design. Since most of these helmets made it impossible to recognize the wearer, it became the custom to fit the helmet with a crest. Some were of beaten bronze and took the form of 'ears', great, sweeping curves, or simpler shapes; others were fashioned from horsehair.

Body armour was used extensively by the Greeks and ranged from fairly simple arrangements of plates to skilfully shaped corselets fitting closely to the body. From earliest times the Greek warrior used close-fitting, bronze greaves to protect the lower part of his legs.

Greek swords

Greek warriors used many weapons, but the sword was not considered the most important among them. For many years the hoplite with his long spear regarded the sword as a reserve weapon to be used only in the last resort. Swords of Mycenae were made of bronze and had long, thin blades which probably made them rather unwieldy. Early examples were often inlaid with gold and decorated with ivory. By about 1500 BC more unsettled times had produced a practical, short-bladed weapon whose blade was fitted with horned or cruciform projections to serve as a hand-guard. By the sixth century BC most troops were carrying a short sword in a sheath below the left arm.

Macedonian infantry carried short stabbing swords, but during the sixth century BC a curved, single-edged slashing sword known as the *kopis* was introduced. It somewhat resembled the modern Ghurka *kukri*, with the blade widening

The Boeotian helmet offered protection with minimum inconvenience to sight and hearing.

Long, shaped cheek-pieces distinguished the Thracian helmet from other Greek helmets.

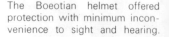

near the top to ensure maximum weight at the cutting point. The *kopis* was used with a slashing stroke delivered from above the left shoulder and was a deadly weapon, as the Spartans demonstrated at Thermopylae.

Late Greek warrior

Many Greeks found that helmets of the Corinthian and Chalcidian shapes interfered with their sight and hearing. Xenophon recommended the type known as Boeotian, which depended on a down-drooping brim for facial protection rather than the nasal and earflaps found on earlier helmets. By the fourth century BC most body armours were unlike earlier ones, being close fitting and often embossed with raised representations of muscles. The legs were protected by close-fitting greaves, and some hoplites had extra pieces to protect the ankles and arms.

(*Above left*) a curved, slightly widened blade made the *kopis* a useful slashing weapon.
(*Above right*) many hoplites used a cruciform-shaped sword.
(*Right*) a late Greek warrior equipped for battle in close-fitting corselet, greaves, and helmet, holding a shield which bears a typical decoration.

Etruscans

Who the Etruscans were and where they came from is almost as much a mystery now as it was in Roman times. Even their language is unlike any other and has defied all efforts at translation. It was most probably from the Orient that they came to settle in Italy, perhaps from Asia Minor. They formed a loose conglomeration of cities, each largely autonomous, and it is from the tombs of cities like Tarquinii and Velutonia that most of our knowledge about the Etruscans has been derived. Ironically, it was the work that the Etruscans put into developing the site of Rome that was responsible for the ascendancy of that town and its citizens, and eventually for the subjugation of Etruria by the Romans themselves. Greeks and Carthaginians both influenced Etruscan development, which, in turn, laid the foundations for many later Roman institutions, not least the military might of Imperial Rome.

It seems likely that the Etruscans were essentially a maritime power, but warriors figure frequently in their tomb paintings and on pottery, and a number of examples of their arms and armour have been excavated. They wore a bronze helmet rather like a modern crash helmet and many of the paintings show it fitted with large, rather impractical crests, but whether these were ever used in battle is open to doubt.

Their body defences were of the type known as scale armour, which is made up by lacing together overlapping

Roman legionary's bronze helmet with typical peak but lacking cheek-pieces, worn before the first century AD (*see page 20*).

A few more elaborate, decorated helmets have survived, but they were primarily parade pieces for they are of very thin metal.

Rome fought the Etruscans for her existence and later developed her famed legions of professional soldiers and officers.

metal plates. This was a simple form of protective garment which was more effective against slashes than determined thrusts. It was a style of armour apparently favoured by the Assyrians, and it has been used in a variety of styles throughout the world, including Japan.

Etruscans appear to have relied, like the Greeks, more on the spear than the sword, and most warriors are depicted carrying two spears with large, leaf-shaped heads. Swords, when carried, are shown as short and also rather leaf shaped. It is perhaps no coincidence that the Roman legions relied heavily on the effect of a barrage of javelins to demoralize the enemy before advancing with their short swords.

Romans

For many centuries the Roman army was the supreme military force in the then known world; it was efficient, well trained and, with a few exceptions, well officered. At first it was essentially a citizens' army, with all true Romans being involved. Their equipment and role were determined by wealth. The richest were equipped with shield, breast-plate, greaves, helmet, sword, and spear, whereas less wealthy men omitted the breast-plate. Poor men had only a helmet; still poorer men had no armour at all and carried only a spear and sword. Slings and stones were the equipment of the poorest of all, who also supplied the trumpeters and horn blowers.

Tactics were based on the legion, apparently introduced in the latter part of the fourth century BC. In place of the solid phalanx the troops were arranged in three lines: the *hastati* in front, next the *principes*, and last the *triarii*. *Hastati* were the prime fighters, armed with javelins and spears and carrying a large, rectangular wood-and-leather shield, the *scutum*; they also wore body armour. This rank engaged the enemy, but if unsuccessful it retired leaving the *principes*, seasoned, well-trained soldiers, to continue the battle, whilst the *triarii* knelt and positioned their long spears to form a strong defensive line. If the *principes* failed to break the enemy or were forced to retreat, the rear rank had to complete the task. A small group of cavalry (about 300) was attached to each legion (about 3,000 men).

Organization and tactical use of the legion were to vary over the centuries from the creation of the Republic to the fall of the Empire. There were corresponding changes in weapons, but for many centuries the legionary was equipped with the *gladius* and *pilum*, whilst wearing body armour and carrying a *scutum*. The *gladius*, which had a blade about two feet long and two inches wide, apparently originated in Spain. The *pilum* was a throwing spear with a small point at the end of a long, soft-iron shaft which, in turn, was fastened to a wooden haft. Mail and scale armour were used, but the *lorica segmentata*, made of carefully designed and cunningly arranged strips of metal, was worn by the majority of the legionaries. Helmets were of bronze, sometimes reinforced with iron, and most had some form of neck-guard, peak, and earflaps.

For serious fighting the legionary relied on his short sword (*above*), the *gladius*, his throwing spear (*right*), the *pilum*, and a great shield (*far right*), the *scutum*. For the business of triumphs and parades he had elaborate helmets complete with full face-masks (*below*).

Gauls

Although the Romans fought many battles against semi-naked barbarians some of their opponents, such as the Gauls, did wear helmets or armour. Their helmets were either functional, with a plain bowl and small peak, or else decorative, drawn up to a rather exaggerated point or having a pair of horns and a crest in the shape of a wheel. Mail was worn by the wealthier Gauls, and by Britons, but the majority wore no armour except perhaps, a leather jerkin. Their shields were usually oval in shape, but some were rectangular, with a slight waist. From their enemies the Romans learned the use of cavalry and of their long-bladed, double-edged swords fitted with simple hand-guards and wooden or horn grips.

Standard bearers (*right*) always led against the Gauls (*above*).

Gladiators

Bread and circuses were traditionally the means of keeping the mobs of Rome happy, and gladiatorial combats were always popular. Fights were arranged between a wide variety of combatants – men against beasts or dwarfs against women – but it was the trained gladiators who aroused audiences to greatest enthusiasm. *Bestiarii* were made to fight lions, tigers, and many other exotic animals. *Retiarii* used tridents and nets and fought without armour, relying on speed and skill to elude their armoured opponents. *Mirmillones* were quite heavily armoured, having a large helmet (fitted with a wide peak, a high comb, and a visor which completely covered the face) and armour on the left arm; they carried shields and swords.

The Roman spectacle often included captives using their native weapons, so that a gladiator (*left*) might find himself opposing a Briton with a fine bronze shield as here.

SAXONS AND VIKINGS
Saxon warrior

The Saxons came originally from what is now northern Germany and Denmark, and they were raiding the English coast during Roman times. Tradition states that they first came to Britain as mercenaries, hired by an English king to drive back the marauding Picts from the north. However that may be, the Saxons eventually settled in Britain and created their own petty kingdoms, often at war with each other.

Their defensive equipment was a shield, usually round, decorated and strengthened by a metal rim and boss. Those helmets which have survived are almost all of high quality and were certainly the property of rulers and nobles. Some, like that from Sutton Hoo, are conical, with face-guards and neck-guards which are decorated with gilding and silver wire applied to suggest features. Body armour was often of mail, but there is strong evidence to suggest that strips of metal were incorporated with the mail to give extra strength.

Saxon armour as elaborate as the Sutton Hoo helmet was rare.

Saxon weapons

Saxon swords were of basic design and had a simple hilt, but a great deal of skill was involved in the production of the double-edged, straight blade. The surface was patterned with a series of lines running up the centre, and these were produced during the complex hammering and twisting of the metal which formed the blade. Hard cutting edges were welded to the core, and the whole blade was then ground and polished. Most blades were about three feet long and two inches wide.

A smaller, dagger-like weapon was the *seax* or *scramasax*, and this had a single-edged blade, the length of which varied considerably. Some swords and *seaxes* had words or symbols engraved on the blades, although this was not common practice until the ninth century. Spears were used both for throwing and thrusting, and the head varied with the purpose of the weapon – those that were thrown were small and light, whereas those for thrusting were large and sometimes barbed. Axes were also used as weapons.

Saxon shields, axes, and swords were often well decorated.

Vikings sometimes wore visored helmets such as the seventh century example on the right and fought with swords and axes. But one of their most important possessions was the long ship, along whose sides the rowers hung their shields to form a protective wall. In these broad, shallow craft crews of raiders crossed great seas and reached lands as far apart as Britain and Russia.

Vikings

In their longships the Vikings took trade and terror to almost every country in Europe and many in Africa and Asia. At first their ships kept near the coast, but soon their skill and courage enabled them to venture across miles of open sea. They came from Sweden, Norway, and Denmark, and their first recorded attack on Britain was in 787 AD, when the crews of three ships sacked the town of Poole. They left, but later they were to return in large numbers.

A great host of Danish raiders roamed Britain, plundering and killing, until they were defeated by Alfred the Great in 878. The Danes fought with weapons very similar to those of the Saxons. Shields were still round and made of leather-covered wood, reinforced with metal. On the back was one strap through which the user passed his hand to grasp a bar at the centre. A hole was cut at the centre of the shield to accommodate the clenched hand, and to guard the hand a raised dome, the shield boss, was secured over the hole. Most of these bosses were quite plain, but some like that from the Sutton Hoo ship were rather elaborate.

27

Viking equipment

Many of the Viking warriors relied solely on their shields, but their leaders, no doubt, wore a byrnie, a coat of mail. These byrnies had short sleeves and usually reached only to the waist, although some were long enough to reach to the knees. A few may have been strengthened by the addition of metal plates, but it is not clear exactly how these were made. Helmets were not uncommon, and many were surmounted by a figure of a boar. Many helmets were conical with a wide brim, and it seems that often some kind of badge was painted on the front to assist recognition. Despite a romantic belief that all Viking helmets were decorated with wings or horns, there is only scanty evidence that such helmets were ever used.

Viking swords were cleverly designed for easy use in action, and this was achieved by tapering the blade towards the point – it meant that there was less weight at the point, so permitting freer movement. This type of blade was common to the majority of Viking swords, but the style of hilt varied considerably, and as many as nine have been identified. Most have a simple cross-guard, either straight or slightly drooping, and it was in the pommel that there were so many variations.

Popular with Vikings, and later with Normans, was the simple, conical helmet with a straight nasal to guard the face.

The straight-bladed Viking sword was for slashing; a single-edged *seax* (*bottom*) was also popular.

Viking axes

Although the Vikings were expert swordsmen they did not eschew other weapons such as spears and axes. The spears of the Saxons and Vikings, used both for thrusting and throwing, had a shaft of ash about seven feet long. One end was tipped with iron, and the leaf-shaped head fitted on the other by means of a long socket which had two side bars. Since the spear was a favourite hunting weapon these bars served to prevent too deep a penetration into wild boar and other prey.

Even more deadly was the great, two-handed Danish axe; the wedge-shaped head with its curved edge was fitted to the end of a six-foot haft. Swung in great arcs, the cutting power of such a weapon must have been terrifying. This Danish axe was a favourite weapon of the housecarls, an élite group of warriors who guarded their king and constituted the core of the Saxon army at Hastings. In battle they formed a line with shields touching edge to edge to create a defensive wall.

ELEVENTH CENTURY

Normans

Some of the Danish sea rovers sailed up the Seine and captured the town of Rouen, making it their headquarters and settling in the surrounding countryside. Charles, the ruler of Gaul, recognized that they could not be evicted and made a treaty with them, ceding the area to these Northmen, Normans, in return for their allegiance to him. The contract was sealed by the marriage of the King's daughter Ghisela and the Danish leader Rollo who, according to one account, agreed to the marriage on hearing that she was of suitable height. Rollo was acclaimed Duke of Normandy, his descendants extended their hold on the north of France, and their lands became known as Normandy. It was from this stock that William, Duke of Normandy, sprang, being confirmed in his title at the age of seven when his father Robert made a pilgrimage to Jerusalem.

On the Bayeux Tapestry Norman archers are shown using short bows, and accounts of the Battle of Hastings stress their great use of this weapon. Some archers are shown wearing mail hauberks (*left*), whilst others lack any armour. During the latter part of the eleventh century there was a gradual increase in the use of the crossbow (*below*).

Cavalry formed the main arm of the Norman forces, and the knights, clad in mail from head to knee, fought with lance, sword, and club and guarded themselves with long, kite-shaped shields.

Mailed knights

The Danes, after landing from their ships, had frequently rounded up all the available horses and turned themselves into cavalry. The Normans developed this form of warfare to such an extent that when William Duke of Normandy landed in England in October 1066 the most important section of his army was composed of mailed cavalry. These knights, mounted on small horses, were covered from head to knee with mail, and their heads were also protected by conical helmets fitted with single-bar nasals. For extra protection they carried a kite-shaped shield, and this was sufficiently large to cover the rider from neck to toe.

In battle these knights fought with sword, mace, and lance. Their legs were usually left unprotected, but on their feet they wore simple, pointed prick-spurs. Most contemporary illustrations show an outline on the chest, but it is not at all clear what this represented; it may have been a reinforcing plate or section of mail.

Military architecture

After Hastings English resistance crumbled and William proceeded to London, where he was crowned as King of England. However, he still had to safeguard his new possessions. At strategic points his lords built their castles, which were of the simple, basic, motte-and-bailey type. A huge, circular ditch was dug and the excavated earth was piled up into a great mound at the centre. At the top of the mound a wooden wall encircled a simple, wooded hall, and here dwelt the constable who commanded the troops. A wooden palisade guarded a pathway down the side of the mound to a simple drawbridge which spanned a ditch encircling a second open space, the bailey, on which were huts, stores, and stables for the troops.

Many of these simple castles were allowed to decay as the danger of English rebellion receded, but some, at specially important sites, were developed by the substitution of stone walls and towers. A number of the mottes, or castle hills, are still to be seen in places such as Windsor.

Although London was not then the capital of England, its

The Normans erected motte-and-bailey castles, with wooden walls.

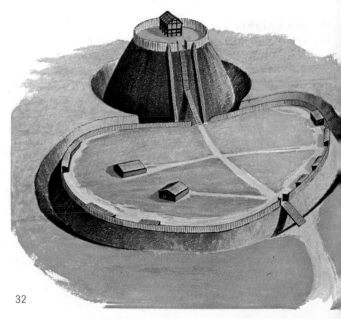

The present White Tower has its origins in William I's reign.

position made it extremely important both in the civil and military sense. William was bound to fortify the town, and he chose as his site one which the Romans had used as a strong point at the eastern corner of the city wall. Work no doubt began soon after his coronation, and by 1078 the great square block of the White Tower was completed. Its building was probably supervised by the designer, who was, in fact, the Bishop Gundulf of Rochester. This priestly architect was also responsible for part of the great Norman castle at Rochester.

Despite its strength the tower apparently suffered some damage from the elements, for it had to be repaired during the reign of William II. This monarch also built a wall around the great keep, conscripting some of London's citizens for the task. Despite sundry alterations carried out over the centuries, such as the widening of windows, the great square keep still conveys most powerfully the solidity of this type of Norman military architecture, with massive walls and tiny windows intended to keep out arrows and other missiles.

TWELFTH CENTURY

Swords

There was little real difference between the sword of the Norman warrior and that of his ancestors, the Danes or Vikings. All used their swords primarily as slashing weapons, although the Normans increasingly used the point in combat. The blade was fairly long and tapered slightly to the point, and its weight was reduced by the cutting of a shallow groove centrally along its length. This groove, known as the fuller, is often erroneously described as a blood gutter. Some of the earlier blades bore a maker's name inset in large letters.

Protection for the hand was afforded by a cross-guard at the top of the blade; it had arms, quillons, normally straight but occasionally slightly down curving. From the centre top of the blade projected a narrow extension called the tang, and around this were secured two strips of wood, tightly bound in position by cord or leather thonging. To balance the weight of the blade and ensure easy handling, a weight, the pommel, was secured at the end of the tang. Pommels varied considerably and offer useful evidence in dating swords. Many of them were simply a semi-circular block fitted to a T-bar at the end of the tang. Norman swords tended to have longer, straighter guards than the earlier examples, and the pommel was less like a recumbent D and more like a brazil-nut in shape. All available evidence suggests that the Norman swords were designed for use in one hand and that the hilts offering room for a two-handed grip were a later development.

When not in use the sword was housed in a scabbard which hung at the side, normally the left, secured by a belt and straps. Some illustrations show the scabbard worn under the mail, in which case the hilt projected through a slit in the side. Scabbards were made from two strips of wood covered with leather and strengthened at the mouth by a metal guard, and at the tip was a more elaborate guard known as the chape.

Many examples of these swords have survived, and such weapons figure prominently in the battle scenes on the Bayeux Tapestry, although the majority of horsemen are shown wielding spears. Swords were to change little until the 1500s when hilts and blades became more elaborate.

Normans used, among others, the Viking sword with its straight cutting blade and quillons. Pommels were more varied in shape.

Bayeux devices

The Norman kite shield was fitted on the inside with short straps for holding and a longer one which could be used to sling the shield over the back when not in use. All the mounted Normans depicted on the Bayeux Tapestry are shown with this typical, long, kite-shaped shield, and each shield bears some form of decoration. In some cases it is no more than a band of colour around the edge; in others it is a series of dots which may represent nails or rivets, or may be purely decorative. Many show far more elaborate patterns; crosses are very common, and some bear dragons or other mythical creatures. Even if we accept the tapestry as true representation rather than artistic interpretation, it does not prove that the use of such patterns and pictures was anything other than decorative and haphazard. Heraldry is, above all, a regulated code, and heraldic arms are inherited; there is no evidence to suggest that the Normans observed either point. Shield faces were, of course, obvious places for displaying arms long after shields had been abandoned on the battlefield.

On many of the shields shown on the Bayeux Tapestry there are patterns and animal shapes, but they are not truly heraldic.

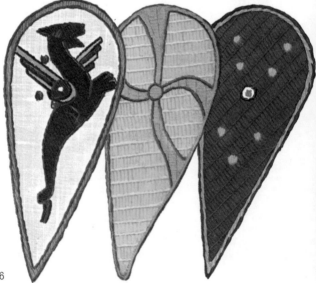

The lion *motif* on the shield and helmet of the figure on Richard I's great seal is one of the earlier examples of true heraldry.

Beginnings of heraldry

Increasing protection by armour and helmets raised certain problems, for it became difficult to distinguish friend from foe as the face was gradually more and more obscured. Eventually facial recognition became impossible, and it was necessary to establish identity by other means, hence the beginnings of heraldry. Earlier races such as the Greeks, Romans, and Normans had used symbols and effigies to aid identification, but their use seems to have been haphazard, and it is not until the twelfth century that anything like a formal system of heraldry appears.

One of the earliest examples of a recognizable coat-of-arms is that shown on the seals of Richard I (1189-99). Both seals feature lions on the shield. However, much more interesting is the placing of the lions on the crest worn on top of the helmet, which, following contemporary fashion, completely covered the face. It may safely be assumed that the use of such badges had been well established for some time before Richard's reign, and here may be seen the beginnings of the complicated science of heraldry.

A broad band from top left to lower right is known as a bend.

Horizontally crossing the centre of the shield is the fess.

Scottish heraldry favours the St Andrew's cross, the saltire.

Heraldic shields

From the design point of view the long kite shield is awkward, and for heraldry its shape was altered to a more triangular form with greater width and less length – a shape often likened to the base of a pressing iron. More elaborate is the *ecusson à bouche*, which has a notch in the top corner, originally to accommodate the lance. The Tudor shield is squarer, whereas the Jacobean shield is florid in the extreme. There were other types of shield as well, and all were divided into nine sections in order that the description, blazoning, of arms could be accurate, although in English heraldry two of the sections were very seldom used.

One point of confusion in heraldry is undoubtedly that the sides of a shield are defined as if seen by the holder; hence the right hand (dexter in correct terminology) appears on the left when seen from the front. All the signs and devices used have their correct heraldic description; thus a broad band crossing the shield diagonally from the top left-hand corner, dexter chief, to the lower right, sinister base, is known as a bend. A broad band crossing the shield horizontally is defined as fess, and two diagonal bands producing a St Andrew's cross are designated saltire. The conventional cross is officially a Greek cross and can be used with a number of variations in detail – over three hundred are accepted by the heraldic authorities! There are also strict rules set down about the combining of charges.

Although the origins of heraldry were largely practical, it soon became a complicated and involved science. As time passed and families inter-married, the arms became more and more concerned with, and complicated by, distinctions for various members of the family. Some symbols acquired a special significance; for example illegitimacy was indicated by the baton sinister, often described erroneously as the bend sinister. Despite the numerous variations produced it was still possible for two families to claim the use of identical, or similar, arms. To settle such disputes a special body of officials was created in the mid-fourteenth century, and today the College of Arms in London is the supreme authority on all matters heraldic.

A conventionally shaped cross is known as the Greek cross.

Division of the shield in this style is called wavy or *ordée*.

This is the baton sinister, a symbol indicating illegitimacy.

Mail

Mail was a versatile form of body defence, although its construction was a long and tedious business. First, the metal was drawn out into wire, wrapped around a former, and cut into open-ended circles. In European mail, each link was then interwoven with adjoining links and the ends were flattened, drilled, and riveted together.

Mail coats, fitted with short sleeves and extending from neck to waist or knee, were highly prized by the Vikings, and sagas such as *Beowulf* make frequent reference to them. The coat of mail, usually referred to as the hauberk or byrnie, was carefully shaped in much the same way as a piece of knitting, with increases and decreases in the number of links. In the majority of cases the links were so arranged that each one was connected to four others. One great advantage of mail was its flexibility: it was supple enough to allow movement with little or no hindrance.

Beneath the mail the knight wore some form of padded garment to afford extra protection and prevent the rings chafing and catching on his skin or undergarments. Not only was the knight's body encased in mail, but a mail hood, the coif, was used to give protection to the head. Later, mail sleeves were lengthened and the ends modified to form a pair of hand coverings known as mufflers. Legs were also protected by mail, either in the form of strips of mail tied on to cover the front of the legs or 'stockings' of mail which were probably held in place by straps.

Mail was not without its disadvantages, not the least being its weight, which pressed mainly upon the shoulders. With a strong blow from a sword or lance there was also a danger of

Mail was a main form of defence for many centuries and was made up of a series of interlocking rings of metal. Each link was usually arranged to join with four surrounding ones. The ends of the links were flattened, drilled, and then riveted together, the whole forming a flexible metal defence.

links splitting and being pushed into the skin, resulting in a possibly mortal septic wound. The only easy way of strengthening the mail was to use thicker rings, but this rendered the mail less flexible. However, despite these quite significant drawbacks mail was to remain a common form of defence until the late seventeenth century.

Mail and scale defences were often combined and during the eleventh and twelfth centuries extended to cover most of the body.

Helmets

Norman helmets were delightfully functional, lacking all unnecessary 'frills' and designed to afford maximum protection. There were two varieties of simple, conical helmet worn over the coif – one hammered from a single piece of metal and perhaps reinforced with a band around the brim, and the other fashioned from a number of sections, with joints reinforced and covered by metal ribs. A nasal, a bar projecting down from the brim, gave some protection from a slash to the face. According to contemporary accounts William had to raise his helmet during the Battle of Hastings to show that he was still alive, and this argues that the nasal was at times large enough to obscure most of the face. A similar bar was sometimes fitted at the back of the helmet to guard the neck.

During the twelfth century some helmets had earflaps fitted, and the neck-guard was made larger. Towards the end of the century a number of styles were in use, including some helmets with a rounded or flat top. Both must have been rather unsatisfactory for, unlike the conical type, there was no glancing surface to deflect a blow.

Facial protection had been increased at the end of the eleventh century when a face-guard, cut with slots for sight

Instead of the conical Norman helmet the twelfth-century knight sometimes wore a flat-topped helmet with a nasal (*below*). The face-protecting plates increased in size until they joined the neck-guard to form a tubular helmet (*right*).

The helmet at the top, known as a kettle hat, was worn by troops over many centuries. The helm, which completely covered the head, was made in a variety of styles, one is 'shown on the right, but many still preferred the conical type with a nasal.

and numerous holes for ventilation, was added to the helmet. Here was the beginning of the later helmets which completely covered the head. Another type of helmet was the kettle hat, which derived its name from its fancied resemblance to an upturned cauldron. This type was much simpler than the others and as such was favoured by many, remaining in use, with minor changes in style, for centuries. All these helmets were tied on to the head with laces.

THIRTEENTH CENTURY

Swords

Although the axe, now fitted on shafts about four feet long, was still a popular weapon, the sword held pride of place. It was carried by both cavalry and infantry and, at the beginning of the thirteenth century, had altered but little from that used at Hastings. Blades were slightly longer and had a more pronounced tip, suggesting a greater use of the point. Fullers were usually narrower, an increasing tendency as the centuries passed. Quillons were still most often straight, but some were curved slightly downwards. Pommels were still mostly of the D or brazil-nut shape, but there was an increasing use of circular pommels, and during the last twenty years of the twelfth century many had had their edges bevelled. A number of swords of this period have been discovered, and many of

Swords changed little in the twelfth and thirteenth centuries.

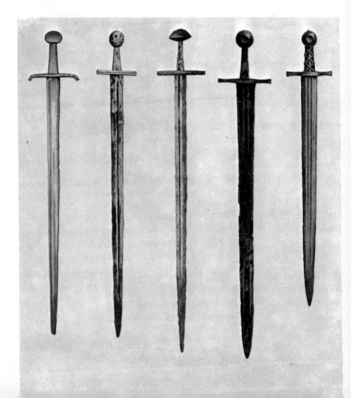

them have the inlaid inscriptions found on earlier swords.

The sword continued to develop as the improvement in armour forced the swordsmith to seek more efficient means of breaking through the knight's defences. To increase the cutting force of a blow the blades were lengthened, and the hilts were made long enough for them to be gripped by both hands. Pommels were now more likely to be wheel shaped, but many variations were used. Another way of breaching the defences was to use a stabbing sword to pierce the links of mail or slip under the unprotected joints of armour, and such weapons had stiff, narrow blades. A third solution offered by the swordsmith was the falchion, which was a shorter sword with a curved, single-edged blade widening towards the tip, thus ensuring that most weight was at the point where the sword edge was most likely to strike home. Daggers were carried by knights, but they were only used as a last resort.

One new variety was the wide-bladed falchion (*second from left*).

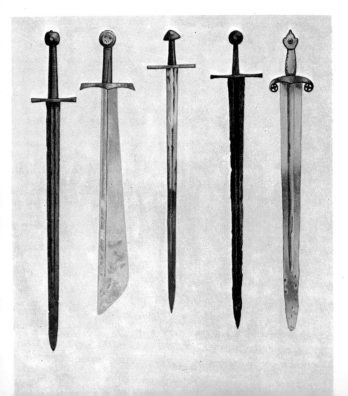

Plate armour

Scale armour was a very old form of defence, and during the thirteenth century long coats of it were sometimes used, although mail was the form of protection worn by most knights. There is evidence that armourers were producing garments, rather like tunics, which were reinforced with plates of metal, and that these were worn over the mail. This coat of plates appeared during the early part of the thirteenth century and continued in use during most of the fourteenth century as well.

Riders' legs were especially vulnerable, and it is not surprising that there were attempts to reinforce their defences. Thighs were fitted with padded covers, and around the middle of the thirteenth century small plates were used to cover the knees. Called poleyns, these plates were fitted to the mail chausses or to the quilted thigh-pieces and although quite small at first were soon big enough to encircle the knee. Metal plates were also made to guard the shins.

Armour for the arms followed a similar pattern, and small, circular plates, couters, were fitted at the elbows from about

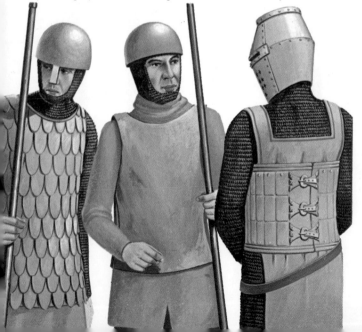

All three soldiers wear mail as the prime defence. They also wear (*left to right*) scale armour, a gambeson, and a coat of plates.

Great helms became more massive and were often reinforced around the eye slits and at the junction of plates (*see page 48*).

1260. It is possible that gutter-like plates were used on the arms, but there is no evidence of this until much later. Protection for the hand, in the form of gauntlets, was also being improved, and such materials as whalebone, brass, and *cuir-bouilli* (leather hardened by treatment with hot wax) were all employed. By the end of the thirteenth century gauntlets entirely of metal plates were certainly in use.

At the end of the thirteenth century there appeared a plate defence for the neck, a gorget, which extended up as far as the nose and down over the shoulders. Most of the plate armour of the thirteenth century was worn only by mounted knights. The infantry wore much simpler protective devices such as the hauberk with long sleeves and a coif. Some wore shorter coats of mail which were known as haubergeons, but many had only a padded tunic, a gambeson, and possibly a simple helmet such as a kettle hat.

Knights

Knights of the thirteenth century were guarded from head to foot by a collection of protective garments including padding, mail, and plate. Upon his head the knight wore a tight-fitting, padded cap covered with a metal coif which was fitted with a strip of mail, the aventail, to cover the chin. Over this went the helmet, which could be a kettle hat or a round-topped helmet with a nasal. For greater protection the knight wore a great helm, which, being cylindrical, completely encircled the head. It was flat topped and had slits for sights, the edges of which were reinforced with bars; to facilitate breathing, small holes were drilled in the lower front section. The body was encased in layers of padded garments and mail, with the possible addition of plate at elbows, knees, and throat, and on the gauntlets. Over all went the long tunic known as the surcoat, which may also have been reinforced with plates. Some knights also wore over the hauberk a body defence known as the cuirie, made of *cuir-bouilli*.

From about 1250 horses were protected by two curtains of mail reaching halfway down the legs and covering the neck and head. Such loose mail must have been heavy and restrictive. Since both rider and horse were now well covered it was imperative that some form of recognition be worn, and the use of heraldic devices increased apace, with crests painted on helmets and other flat surfaces, including small plates, ailettes, attached to the shoulders. These were of treated leather, whalebone, and metal and were worn at the end of the thirteenth and beginning of the fourteenth centuries. From a belt hung the scabbard, the fitting of which was so designed as to make the sword hang at an angle.

Sword-belts were elaborately laced to ensure that the sword hung at a comfortable angle.

There was an increasing use of extra reinforcing plates at knees, elbows, and the throat, although mail still predominated. The head was protected by a coif which often covered a metal skull-cap and over all went a kettle hat or great helm. Heraldry was well established, and arms were displayed on shields, ailettes, and surcoats.

Swords

At the end of the thirteenth century swords had already begun to develop into rather specialized forms unlike the earlier stabbing weapons. They were also becoming less the weapon of the nobility. Many were longer and heavier, to increase the force now required to make any impression on the greatly improved body defences of the knights. Grips tended to be longer, affording room for the two-handed swing with its greater force. Swords with long, stiff, narrow blades were produced, and these were intended to pierce the mail by concentrating the thrust on a small area. It was fashionable to secure a chain from the sword-hilt to the belt or, later, to a staple on the cuirie. Daggers and helmets were similarly protected against loss. Daggers with fairly short, tapering blades were only the last resort in combat and were usually carried on the right-hand side of the belt. Shields were much smaller, and foot soldiers usually carried a buckler.

Greater variety was now common in the details of swords.

Developments begun earlier continued during the fourteenth century and specialized swords became the order of the day; indeed some knights carried two swords. At the belt hung a general-purpose sword with a blade designed for stabbing and slashing and fitted with a straight, or slightly down-curving, cross-guard and a pommel which was wheel or pear shaped. Blades tended to be longer than previously, and to compensate for the extra weight pommels were somewhat larger. Blades tapered gradually to the point and were double edged. Suspended from the saddle was the thrusting sword, with a stiff, narrow blade tapering acutely to the point, which might well be thickened for greater strength. There is evidence that this type of sword was used as a lance, the knight charging with the pommel against his shoulder. In order to obtain a more secure grip on these larger swords the first finger was looped over the cross-guard, and an inch or so of the blade was left blunt; this portion was called the ricasso.

Many swords were made longer, stiffer and used for thrusting.

Other weapons

As well as the sword fourteenth century warriors had a considerable armoury at their disposal, ranging from daggers to longbows. Axes, so popular with the Danes, remained a favourite weapon both with the foot soldier and the knight, who fought on horseback and on foot. For the horseman the axe-head was mounted on a short staff and often had a sharp spike on the back of the blade. For foot combat it was more common for the head to be mounted at the end of a long shaft, and in order to provide extra strength for the handle long metal arms, langets, extended from the head along its sides. The edge of the axe-head was usually curved in order to give as much leverage and cutting power as possible. Like the shorter axes, they were fitted with a spike on the head. Clubs, simple, highly lethal, and ever popular, continued in use. Maces, a type of club, were developing into a form which became common in the fifteenth century. Their heads were composed of a number of flanges arranged around the shaft.

For many of the foot soldiers called from their homes to serve in the feudal levy, their only weapons were those that they took with them, and in many instances these were domestic implements such as pitchforks, flails, or blades mounted on shafts for hedging. Some of the hedging tools were developed into a recognizable weapon, the bill, with a long cutting head and a small, rearward-pointing spike. Lances were used by mounted troops, and a shortened version, some five feet long, was used for foot combat.

It was during the fourteenth century that the English archers first achieved their control of the battlefield. A thick shaft of yew, elm, or ash standing some six feet high and a stout linen string constituted the formidable longbow. The arrows, about three feet long, were of birch and were fitted with goose feathers and a variety of points. Each archer carried a bundle of about two dozen arrows pushed under his belt. With a pull of anything up to one hundred pounds, the longbow demanded constant practice to master its use, but it was deadly up to a maximum range of 400 yards. Crossbows required far less skill and were very powerful, but they were much slower than longbows, which could discharge twelve arrows in the time it took to shoot one crossbow bolt.

Axes and maces (*above and below*) were still commonly used, although the latter now had flanged heads.

Longbows were gaining control on the battlefield, but crossbows were also more powerful and needed mechanical spanning aids: see the windlass (*below*). Bills were still common.

Helmets

The fourteenth century was a period of change, and a number of new types of helmet appeared. Great helms probably varied least of all, but their use was gradually restricted to the tournament instead of war. Some were made with loops at their base which were used to strap the helm in position.

The round-topped helmet of the thirteenth century was improved by making the crown more pointed. A blow from a weapon was now deflected and made to glance off, so that its force was dissipated. This type of helmet, the bascinet, was extended to cover the back of the neck and the sides of the head. At first the bascinet was worn over the coif, but after about 1320 the coif was abandoned and a short mail curtain, the aventail, was fitted to the rim of the helmet. Some bascinets were decorated with a circlet rather like a small crown. Kettle hats were still worn by many mounted and foot troops and, although detail varied, most had a conical crown and a wide brim.

Bascinets became popular, and the great helm (*bottom*) tended to be restricted to tilting.

During this century the moveable face-piece, the visor, appeared, enabling the wearer to bare his face when there was no danger. Some visors were pivoted at the sides of the helmet, whereas others were hinged at the brow. Visors were at first flat, but gradually they became rounded. The sights were no longer mere slits but had surrounding flanges for extra protection. Ventilation holes (it must have been extremely stuffy inside the helmet) were numerous, although sometimes only drilled on the right side of the visor. Some visors were rounded, whereas others had a snouted appearance; helmets with the latter were often called pig-faced bascinets. Bascinet visors were made detachable; like hinges, they were fitted with securing pins which could be withdrawn to release the visor. Bascinets were either worn beneath a great helm without the visor or on their own either with or without the visor. The aventail extended over the shoulders and was secured to the rim of the bascinet by staples and laces.

Face visors were attached to bascinets at the brow or side and could be raised or lowered.

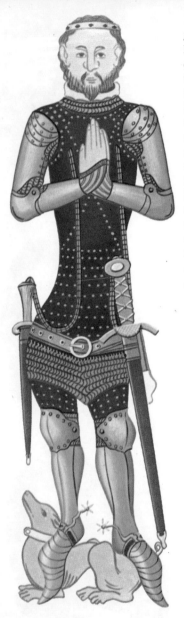

Armour

Plate armour became far more common during the fourteenth century and was extended to all parts of the body. Curved plates were secured to the outside of legs and arms, and the plates at elbow and knee were lengthened to overlap them; eventually all were secured by hinges to form a complete arm or leg defence. Gauntlets, at first of mail, were strengthened by metal plates, the fingers being fitted with individual, small plates which allowed free movement.

Body armour was also being developed, and the most common form was that of metal hoops riveted to a leather garment. There is some evidence to suggest that a small, solid breast-plate was worn by some knights. Hauberks often had a stiffened collar which stood up to protect the neck. Inventories of this period occasionally mention a form of collar called a pizaine, but its exact nature is uncertain. It was possibly a separate collar of stiffened mail. Rigidity was given

Dating from about 1370, this brass of Ralph de Knevynton from Essex shows a skirt of hoops fastened to fabric.

by the use of thick links. Mail was still the prime defence, but it was reinforced by a padded tunic, the aketon, worn beneath it and a coat of plates over it. Over all went the surcoat, now shortened at the front, and the extra plate defences.

Plate armour

Arm-pieces now comprised two plates which completely circled the upper part of the arm, and the shoulder was guarded by a number of shaped metal strips called lames. Similarly, the shin was enclosed within two plates, whilst at the knee the poleyn was fitted with a shaped extension to afford some protection to the back of the joint. Later in the century the thigh was also given plate defences. Metal plates, resembling civilian shoes in shape, guarded the feet.

By 1360 many breast-plates were probably composed of a single plate, whereas the skirt defence was still fashioned out of a number of metal hoops. In some cases the back-plates were dispensed with, and the breast-plate and front skirt were simply secured over the mail with straps crossing at the back. Some of the illustrations of the period also show straps to hold down the aventail of the bascinet. Guard chains were still used occasionally to secure the sword and dagger to the breast-plate as a precaution against loss.

In the fourteenth century mittens of plate (*left*) replaced those of mail. Plate gauntlets appeared (*right*) and from 1375 onwards were quite common. Design improved until one large plate guarded the back of the hand and smaller ones the fingers (*centre*).

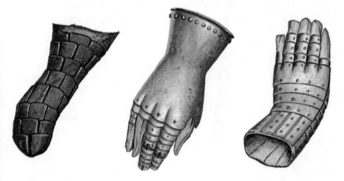

Knights

Armour during the fourteenth century was extremely diverse. As time passed there was a continuing and increasing emphasis on the use of plate armour, but many styles were worn and it must not be assumed that any single fashion was universal. Many knights saw little military service and were content to retain their old-fashioned armour, whilst others, with greater need and more money (for armour was expensive), discarded older pieces and purchased the latest styles. Even with new styles a number of variations could be found; for instance, some knights fought wearing visors, whilst others preferred greater freedom and accepted the greater risk by discarding the visor completely. A variety of helmets was available, and any type might be worn with the armour, including the great helm and the simple kettle hat.

Heraldry was now well established and developed, and its effects were to be seen

Mail, plate, a padded aketon, and a coat of plates make up the defences worn by Sir John de Creke (*c* 1325); by this date many knights were carrying a much smaller shield.

in many walks of life. Early in the fourteenth century the ailettes were discarded, but the practice of carrying banners was still observed by many knights. Some knights adopted a tight-fitting tunic on which was embroidered their coat-of-arms, and some had the tunic padded as well, so that it afforded a little extra protection. There was an increase in decorative fashions, and an elaborate, jewelled belt began to be worn fastened across the hips. Towards the end of the century the sword and dagger were attached to this belt, probably with small hooks.

Some of the nobles had their armour decorated with engravings or edgings of gold, silver, and brass. There are numerous contemporary references to decorations of velvet and precious stones, but few examples, if any, have survived. Most of the evidence for the study of armour of this period is drawn from brasses, effigies, and manuscripts; actual examples are extremely rare.

Arm defences were fairly well developed by about 1325, as shown on this brass of Sir William Fitzralph from Essex. Mail still predominates, but plate is becoming more popular.

FIFTEENTH CENTURY
Helmets

In Italy a style of helmet closely resembling the ancient Greek Corinthian appeared, although it seems to have been abandoned by about 1470. Known as the *barbuta*, it had a smooth skull, which was extended to the shoulders, and at the front was a T-shaped opening for the nose and eyes. A similar *barbuta* had a simpler, wider facial opening; this form survived until the end of the century.

Another, far more complex helmet which apparently originated in Italy was the armet (see page 62). For the tournament, knights still favoured a version of the great helm; as the lower lip of the sight projected forward it gained the name of frog-mouthed helmet. The projecting lower lip was designed in such a way that when the knight was seated upright it was so positioned as to prevent any blade entering.

Bascinets dating from the early part of the fifteenth century which show some of the many possible variations of this type.

Although the kettle hat seems to have fallen from favour in Italy during this century, this certainly was not the case in Germany, where it was as popular as ever. Many had small crowns and deeply down-drooping brims from which a section had been cut to allow the wearer to see. With the kettle hat the knight often wore a bevor, a shaped plate guarding the lower face, the neck, and the top of the chest.

Sallets were also popular in Germany and were often distinguished by a long, laminated, pointed tail to guard the neck. At the front, half or full visors were fitted. Late in the fifteenth century there appeared a German sallet which had a very short tail and a closer-fitting skull; a flat visor, pierced with slits, completed the helmet. Great bascinets were common in Germany; these had the aventail replaced by solid plates and were normally fitted with a hinged visor. The large, rounded helmet was fastened to the body armour by straps which held it rigid, not moving with the head.

The hinged visors fitted to bascinets were extremely varied in shape, but all had numerous, very necessary ventilation holes.

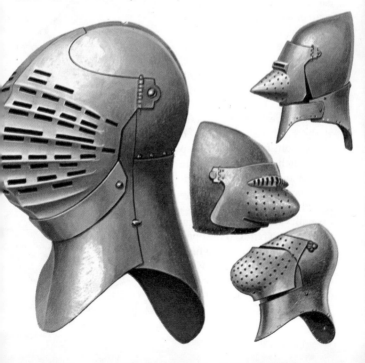

Armets

Bascinets were long to serve the knight, but armourers of the fifteenth century were, no doubt, seeking newer and more convenient types of helmet. One style, the armet, probably originated in Italy and was to be adopted and modified all over Europe. It was first illustrated early in the century in Bavaria on a German effigy of a knight who died in 1416, and by the middle of the century it was not uncommon. Basically it consisted of a skull, usually rounded, very rarely pointed, which was extended to about ear level. From the back a strip of metal extended downwards as far as the neck, following the shape of the head. Two shaped cheek-pieces, hinged at the top to the skull, could be closed to cover the entire face. These side plates slightly overlapped the 'tail' at the back and were locked at the front by a catch. A gap of an inch or so allowed the wearer to see; on a few armets this space was left unprotected, but on most there was a small visor, pivoted at the sides, which reduced the open gap to a minimum at which clear vision and safety were compatible; many visors could be detached from the

1

3

5

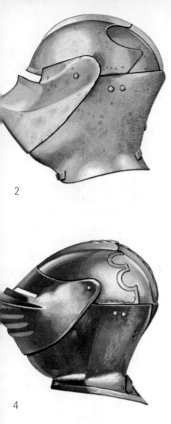

2

4

Helmets from Italy and Germany show how the pieces of an armet fit together. Hinged to the skull were two cheek-pieces (1). Pivoted at the side was a visor and secured to the crown was a strengthening plate (2-4). A wrapper, sometimes lengthened by gorget plates, was strapped on below the visor (5). Origin of the examples: 1 Italian (*c* 1430); 2 Milanese (*c* 1440); 3 Italian (*c* 1475); 4 Italian (*c* 1550); 5 Innsbruck (*c* 1505).

helmet simply by removing the hinge pins.

Extra protection for the face was obtained by a shaped piece of armour, the wrapper, which was strapped on to cover the front of the helmet below the visor. A strap encircling the neck was protected at the back by a large, decorative rondel fitted at the bottom of the tail. At the top of the wrapper there was a small slot which accommodated a bar projecting from the side of the visor; this served as a convenient handle for raising and lowering the visor. Some wrappers were lengthened by the addition of a few gorget plates which extended down to protect the chest. Greater strength for the brow of the helmet was obtained by a shaped plate permanently secured to the skull, and around 1460 the top of the latter was ridged slightly, again to give extra strength.

As the century went on the face opening became progressively larger – a trend which reached its peak with the close helmets. German armets produced early in the sixteenth century had wider tails and cheek-pieces hinged, not at the top, but at the back of the side plates.

Knights

During the early fifteenth century two distinct styles of armour were developed – one originating in Italy and the other in Germany. Both styles had certain peculiarities, but each influenced the other and they were often combined.

The Italian armour, produced at Milan and Pisa, tended to have smooth, rounded outlines with rather large shoulder defences, pauldrons, curving over to give a 'chunky' appearance. Extra plates were often added to the shoulder defences, and the poleyns at the knees and the couters at the elbows were curved round to afford maximum protection. Breastplates were of two overlapping plates, allowing the wearer some flexibility of movement. Since the lance was held under the right arm the plates on this side of the armour were specially shaped to take it. From about 1380 a lance-rest was a common feature; this was a bracket fitted on the right side of the breast-plate, and it was intended to take the shock of the blow when the lance struck its target. On the fifteenth-century Italian armours this lance-rest was detachable, secured by a pin and a series of bars. From the lower edge of the breast-plate hung a series of hoops forming the fauld, and from the bottom of these hung another plate, the tasset. Other refinements included the raised rib placed at the tip of the thigh-pieces and at the edge of the breast-plate, around the neck and armholes. This served to deflect the point of a weapon sliding over the surface of the armour.

Outside Germany the Italian style was now generally used, although there were variations in detail. The armours of English knights during the early part of the fifteenth century had an almost smooth outline with a breast- and back-plate hinged on the left and secured on the right by straps. A skirt of hoops hung around the waist, the arms were completely enclosed in plates, and the hands were encased in plate gauntlets. To guard the armpits, always vulnerable and yet difficult to protect, small metal discs were attached to the shoulders. Mail was also used for protection, and beneath his armour the knight wore an arming doublet, a padded garment with patches of mail stitched on at vulnerable points. In donning his armour the knight worked from the feet upwards, leaving the gauntlets and helmet to the last.

Italian armours showing the change from the late fourteenth (*left top and bottom*) to the mid-fifteenth century (*right*).

The second type, the German, was one of the most attractive styles of armour ever produced. It first began to develop around 1460 and continued to be popular until the end of the century, although it underwent minor modifications. This armour, known as Gothic, was produced in Nuremberg, Augsburg, and Innsbruck among others. The style is characterized by an elongated, slender outline and a decoration of points and fluting. The fluting served the double purpose of giving extra strength to the plates and helping to deflect weapon points from vital areas. Many of the pieces were edged with brass. The helmet most often worn was the sallet, and a throat-guard, the bevor, was worn as well.

The breast-plate was like its Italian counterpart, usually of two plates, whereas the top of the shoulder was protected by a series of curved metal plates, spaulders, and the armpit by a besagew. Some armourers tended to exaggerate the style, and some armours had rather grotesque couters with enormous spikes. Gauntlets had rather long, pointed cuffs, bearing the typical, graceful fluting and scalloped edges.

Gothic armour of the late fifteenth century with fine form and graceful outline. (*Opposite*) helmets were the sallet type (*see page 61*), some with laminated neck-pieces (*top*). Gauntlets had long, pointed cuffs and the characteristic curved ridging; both fingered and mitten types were made.

(*Left*) one of the finest of Gothic armours was made at Augsburg (*c* 1480) and belonged to the Archduke Sigmund of Tyrol. (*Above*) a later, simpler form of Gothic armour.

A pivoted arm on the quintain administered a sharp blow to a careless rider — a speedy method of instruction for young squires!

Tournaments

It was not easy for a knight encumbered with mail or other armour to manage a spirited horse and wield a long lance or a sword at the same time; in fact it required practice and training. For those of sufficient standing to be eligible for knighthood, riding was second nature acquired in childhood. Skill at arms had, however, to be learnt. Serving as a squire to a knight taught a youngster the theory of knighthood, but practical experience had to be gained the hard way.

The quintain was a simple, but effective, device to practise on and was made up of a pivoted arm set on top of a pole. At one end of the arm was some form of target, perhaps in the shape of a Turk's head, and at the opposite end a weight was suspended. Charging at the quintain, the rider struck the target with his lance and then had to follow through, avoiding the weight as it swung round; lack of skill meant a hefty clout and a good chance of being unhorsed.

When some degree of competence had been achieved it was time to turn to more active methods and here the *mêlée*, or tournament, played an important part for this was, in effect, a practice war. Large groups of knights took part in these mock battles which could, and did, cover many miles of countryside. On more 'formal' occasions the combat took place in a limited space. Tournaments became great social occasions, with knights travelling quite long distances to participate. Some monarchs viewed them with suspicion as places where rebellion could be plotted and for this reason forbad them unless special permission had been granted. Ordinary or blunted weapons were used in these contests, and for the winners there were opportunities to gain quite handsome prizes given by the organizer, in addition to the right to claim the armour and horse of the vanquished. Great sums of money were expended on these spectacles, and surviving accounts show that often special crests and weapons were purchased.

The tilt which was run with the riders on opposite sides of a wooden barrier so ensuring greater safety (*see page 71*).

Tilt armour

One of the popular pastimes of the nobility during the Middle Ages was that of tilting. In the early days the emphasis had been on mass combat, with groups of knights staging mock battles in the tourney. Many tournaments started as friendly combats, but, as tempers frayed and blows became harder, they changed into small-scale wars with killed and wounded on both sides. This mass combat was gradually replaced by single combat or jousts. Sometimes the weapons were blunted, but often they were the same as those used in war. Since most knights had no desire to lose their lives unnecessarily, heavy armour was developed specially for the joust early in the fourteenth century. Extra pieces of armour were strapped into place, and the vamplate, a hand-guard, was fixed on to the

Special forms of armour were designed for the tilt and tournament. (*Below left and opposite right*) German armours for the *Gestech*. (*Below right*) a foot combat armour from Italy (*c* 1490). (*Opposite left*) an Austrian armour for the *Scharfrennen*.

lance. Shields were also strapped on, and the lance was couched across the horse's neck so that riders charged each other shield to shield.

About 1420 a new style of tilting was introduced; a wooden fence separated the opponents and so reduced the chances of horses colliding. Great helms were still popular for tilting, but in Europe more specialized types of armour were made for different styles of combat.

For *Scharfrennen* (the running tilt with sharp lances), enormous, semi-circular vamplates gave protection to the whole of the right side of the body. The German *Gestech* was fought with blunted or rebated lances which were fitted with three- or four-pronged heads. In this type of combat the aim was either to splinter the lance or unhorse an opponent. Great helms were worn, and a small, wooden shield was laced on to the left side of the body. Since the tilt offered protection for the lower part of the body, it was usual to leave the legs free of armour.

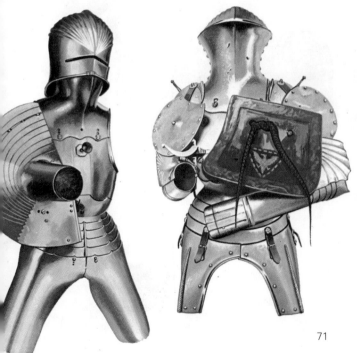

Horse armour

Archaeological and sculptural evidence clearly shows that forms of horse armour were used by heavy cavalry in the later Roman period. Mail trappers, reaching almost to the horse's feet, were worn then, but later their use seems to have been abandoned until the middle of the twelfth century. Even then the only common form was apparently a head defence, the chanfron. Mail defences were in use during the thirteenth century, and there are many references to padded horse armours at that time.

Coats of plate similar to those worn by men were also used. Larger plates of leather and metal were introduced late in the thirteenth century, and one of the first pieces was a peytral, worn on the horse's chest. In the early fourteenth century

Mail was one of the earliest forms of horse armour and was used by the Romans. Plate defences were gradually developed, becoming most common during the fifteenth and sixteenth centuries. Nevertheless, horse armour was very nearly abandoned by the early seventeenth century.

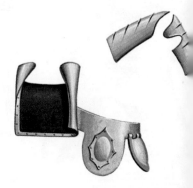

there are references to plates fitted over the rest of the horse's body, flanchards at the side and cruppers at the rear. For the neck a combined piece of mail and plate, known as the crinet, was used. By the fifteenth century the plates were generally larger and more extensive, and in many instances the horse's armour, the bard, was decorated in exactly the same style as that of the knight. During the sixteenth century bards were far more common, and full armours as well as lighter types using smaller chanfrons, often protecting only the top of the head, were popular. Horse armour was gradually discarded during the second half of the sixteenth century, and by the end of the first quarter of the seventeenth century it had largely been abandoned. The chanfron, or rather the half chanfron, and the crinet were the last pieces to go.

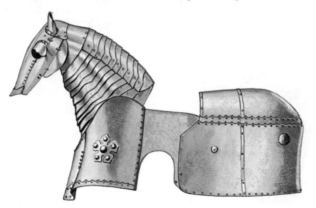

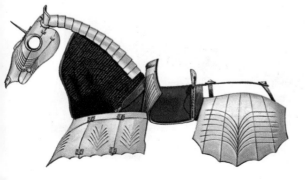

Chanfron and crinet (*see pages 72-3*)

Saddles were sometimes of ivory, like this mid-fifteenth century one from Germany; some were fitted with front plates (*above*) to protect the rider's legs. (*Left*) a chanfron.

Horse equipment

For the mounted knight his horse was of prime importance and represented an expensive piece of equipment. Knights might well own at least three horses: a destrier, the prize steed, a courser for war, and a general riding horse or rounsey.

The saddle differed greatly from the modern riding model, for it was so designed that the rider almost stood in it. It was only with the evolution of the stirrup that a mounted warrior was able to make full use of his height, and this style of riding enabled him to use the sword or mace with the whole force of his body. Saddles were apparently first used by the Goths and probably copied from them by the Romans. The front, the pommel, of a Norman saddle was fairly low and curved forward, whereas the back, the cantle, was slightly taller but curved over in much the same way. As time passed the cantle was heightened and the sides were curved round to enclose the back of the rider. The pommel was also extended and often faced with metal plates to protect the rider's legs. Wood, ivory, leather, and bone were all used in the construction of saddles, and their seats were padded with hay.

Spurs were at first very simple and had a single spike, the prick-spur, on a U-shaped arm which strapped around the foot, but about 1330 another type, with a spiked disc, the rowel, became more general. At first the 'neck' of metal joining the rowel and U-shaped arm was very long, but it was gradually reduced, and in the seventeenth century it had a distinct, downward bend.

Stirrups first appeared in the eighth century AD and made a great difference to the rider, giving him greater purchase and control.

75

Swords and daggers

Although the basic weapon of this period was still the sword designed for slashing and thrusting, its hilt was beginning to acquire some of the loops and bars found on sixteenth- and seventeenth-century weapons. Blades varied in length and width, and it is difficult to generalize. Rigidity was obtained by the use of a central rib or by grinding down the edges to produce a flattened blade, triangular in section. Cross-guards were usually long and often curved towards the blade or, occasionally, into a horizontal S-shape.

Around the middle of the century there appeared an infantry sword on which one of the arms of the hilt curved up to the pommel, thus forming a hand-guard, the knuckle-bow. Pommels were of many types; many were wheel shaped but equally common were those of pear or kite-like form. The practice of hooking a finger over the cross-guard to improve the grip was increasing, and apart from the blunt ricasso there were often down-curving loops on the quillons to protect the first finger. Sword-belts were fairly narrow and were worn at an angle across the hips. The daggers used by the knights at this time were mostly straight, stiff-bladed weapons with the hilt protected by a disc at either end of the grip; they were called rondel daggers.

(*Opposite*) during the fifteenth century the sword hilt began to acquire extra loops and guards and became generally more complex. However, the sword was still basically a cut-and-thrust weapon.

(*Above*) the extremely popular quillon dagger (*see pages 112-3*).
(*Below*) the earlier rondel dagger was more of a military weapon.

Pole-arms and other weapons

During the fifteenth century there was a revival of the pike, especially by the Swiss, who wreaked havoc on their opponents when they first introduced new formations using this very long spear. Switzerland was, at this time, a source of hired troops, and many kings numbered Swiss mercenaries amongst their armies. For the purpose of repelling cavalry charges the pike was ideal, for it had a shaft of ash up to eighteen feet in length and a long, strengthened steel head. With the ranks carefully staggered it was possible to present a solid hedge of steel points sufficient to deter any horseman.

The success of the Swiss tactics using the pike encouraged many other commanders to copy the system, and the pike remained a popular weapon until the seventeenth century. Lances were made so that they were thickest near the grip and tapered away in either direction. A vamplate was fitted around the shaft just in front of the grip. For light cavalry a simpler, straight shaft was more common.

Chivalry had begun to lose its pride of place during

Two early sixteenth-century halberds and a corseque (*right*)

this century, and the foot soldier was already coming to play a more important part in the art of warfare. In order to pierce the strong armour so commonly worn it was necessary to concentrate the force of a hard blow on a small area. A variety of axes and pole-arms were produced, and most had some form of spike which could pierce an armour.

Pole-axes, also known as ravens' bills, were popular and effective, with spikes at both ends of the shaft for thrusting, a hammer-head, and an axe-head. Simpler but not dissimilar was the halberd, which had a spike and an axe-head as well as a spike at the tip. Most staff weapons had long side bars, langets, extending from the head along the shaft, for this gave additional strength to the shaft and also lessened the chances of the head being struck off.

The glaive, a cutting and stabbing weapon which resembled a scythe blade mounted on a shaft about five feet long, was also used by many

Pole-axes and halberds could be used as axes or spears. All feature langets, and one (*far left*) a rondel hand-guard.

79

foot soldiers because it was such a simple weapon. Bills were still used by many, again because they were simple and ready to hand for the peasant called to serve in the feudal levy.

Longbows continued to be weapons of importance throughout the century, and such victories as Agincourt in 1415, when English bowmen slaughtered thousands of French knights, made them feared by all. The archer guarded his wrist against the slap of the bowstring by a leather or horn bracer inside the left wrist.

Arrow-heads were made in a variety of designs, but war arrows had rather narrow points intended to punch through plate armour. Crossbows were made even more powerful by the use of composition and steel bows, but their use was still limited by their slow rate of discharge. However, one new feature which was beginning to play a more and more important part in battle was, of course, gunpowder; its use was spreading and armies were beginning to deploy groups of gunners.

Horsemen made use of their spears and lances, but in addition they had such devices

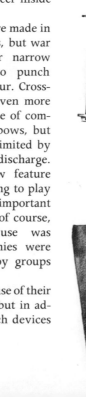

as the war hammer and mace. War hammers were, in effect, miniature pole-axes. A shaft of metal or wood, the latter being strengthened with metal strips, was fitted to a head which had a spike at the tip, a thickened spike at the back, and a four-pointed hammer-head. Below the head was a rondel which gave some protection to the hand. Later varieties of war hammers were fitted with longer, slightly curved spikes and remained in use in eastern Europe after they had been abandoned in the west.

Maces had similar shafts with rondels to protect the hand. Heads were still composed of flanges, often somewhat triangular in shape, again with the purpose of bringing maximum impact to a minimum area. The grips of hammers and maces were often leather covered; when not in use these weapons were hung from the saddle-bow. War hammers could also be used in foot combat, but the mace was only wielded on horseback.

(*This page*) horsemen favoured the war hammer, with its stout pick-point for piercing armour. (*Opposite*) flanged maces (*top*), an early halberd (*bottom left*), and a glaive (*bottom right*).

SIXTEENTH CENTURY
Close helmets

Old-fashioned helmets continued to be worn long after new styles appeared, and during the sixteenth century many helmets popular in the preceding century were still in use. Kettle hats remained popular and, for the wealthier soldiers, armets were still normal wear. In the case of helmets with moveable visors or cheek-pieces, some form of holding device – spring catch, hooks, or screws – was normal from the beginning of the century. Nearly all helmets had larger combs. German armets were often made with a special rim that fitted over a raised ridge on the collar of the armour, so that they were free to rotate but were otherwise firmly in position.

However, the armet was displaced in the sixteenth century by various forms of an outwardly similar helmet, the close helmet. In the armet the face was primarily protected by the hinged side plates, and the visor guarded the slot left for

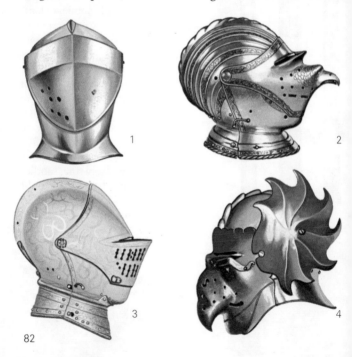

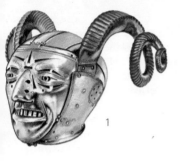

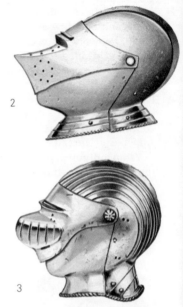

Close helmets replaced the armet during the sixteenth century. Some were specially made for the tilt and some for war; some were extremely grotesque. (*Opposite*) 1 Italian (*c* 1510). 2 German (*c* 1530). 3 German (*c* 1560). 4 German (*c* 1515). (*This page*) German helmets: 1 1511–4; 2 *c* 1545; 3 *c* 1530

vision, but in the close helmet the face was covered by a bevor attached to the helmet in such a way that it could be swung upwards, clear of the face. Pivoted at the same point was a visor which could be moved independent of the bevor; on some helmets the visor was made in two pieces.

To put on the close helmet both visor and bevor were pushed up over the brow, the head was positioned inside the skull, and the bevor then lowered and locked into place, often with a spring catch. When danger became acute the visor could be lowered to cover the face. On some close helmets a fork-like bar was attached to the bevor, so that the visor could be held safely in the open position. The visor was produced in a variety of shapes, including some versions of human or grotesque faces. About 1540 the visor was separated into two parts, and this style became general. Most early close-helmet visors projected forward to a marked degree, but later in the century this feature was much reduced.

During the second quarter of the sixteenth century

gorget plates were often fitted to the necks of close helmets. Many of these helmets were decorated with engraved patterns, and on a few expensive examples there might be some gold inlay work. As with other styles of helmet the inside was lined and padded to reduce the shock from any blows. Close helmets were produced in Italy, Germany, and England.

Maximilian armour

Germany and Italy were the two main armour-producing countries of Europe, with their main centres at Innsbruck, Augsburg, Nuremberg, and Milan. Each country tended to develop individual styles, but each, in turn, was influenced by the other. Early Italian armour tended to be rounded and

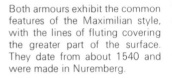

Both armours exhibit the common features of the Maximilian style, with the lines of fluting covering the greater part of the surface. They date from about 1540 and were made in Nuremberg.

plain, whilst Germany had the slender, spiky, Gothic style.

During the first thirty years of the sixteenth century German armourers produced another style, usually known as Maximilian. Its characteristic feature was a series of ridges over the entire surface excepting the greaves, which were always left plain. On early examples the fluting was comparatively wide apart, but later the ribs were closely spaced. Edges of individual items of armour were turned and decorated with a spiral pattern called roping. Many of the Maximilian armours were fitted with mitten gauntlets, which had no individual fingers but a series of plates to guard the back of the hand. Helmets on these armours were often of the bellows type, with a visor which had a series of curved 'steps'.

Maximilian armours were not identical; as with these three (c 1520), the detail varies.

Greenwich armour

Armour was made in England, but little is known about it before Henry VIII's reign. Many European sovereigns had established centres of production, and perhaps Henry felt England should have one too. Production of armour in England had previously been both inferior and insufficient for normal demands. When English nobles required good armour they sent abroad for it, and when large quantities were wanted they too were ordered from abroad. Henry had a small group of armourers from Italy and Belgium working for him at Greenwich, a small village just outside London, and in 1515 he arranged for German and Dutch armourers to join them.

Greenwich armours were for war and the tilt. Two of Henry VIII's suits, dated 1527 (*right*) and 1540 (*left*)

Production at Greenwich continued until the 1640s, but at first the armour produced seems to have been made solely for the king and his friends. Greenwich armours were usually decorated, and a number have been identified from a contemporary album of drawings. All the armours illustrated were probably made there by Jacob Halder.

Henry VIII had several Greenwich armours, including a garniture made in 1540. This consisted of a basic armour and a variety of pieces which could be added to adapt it for certain forms of combat. Greenwich suits are rare; they are recognizable by the shape of the helmet, a wide-shouldered appearance, and a number of other features.

More Greenwich armours: (*left*) Sir Christopher Hatton's (1585); (*right*) Henry VIII's tilt armour (*c* 1515-20)

Hunting

Egyptian wall paintings show many hunting scenes in which the longbow plays a prominent part. Assyrian kings delighted to hunt the lion and chased it in their great war chariots before dispatching it with an arrow. Alexander the Great was a keen hunter and on his campaigns found time to spear wild boar, which were regarded, like lions, as the king's special prey. Spartans also hunted the wild boar.

In Britain the Romans and Saxons do not appear to have been keen hunters, although records indicate that some sport was undertaken. The Normans brought with them a much keener interest in blood sports, and forest laws controlling great areas of country ensured that the king enjoyed good hunting. Under mediaeval protocol animals known as 'beasts of the forests' could only be hunted by the king or people with royal permission. These creatures were certain kinds of deer and the wild boar, of whom it was said 'he could slit a man from knee to breast with one sweep of his tusks'.

To take a charging boar with a spear required nerve and a stout staff, and boar spears had thick staves with strong heads. Some hunted the boar with swords, and these too had thick, strengthened blades. Both spears and swords often had the blade pierced by a cross-bar intended to prevent too deep a penetration by the point. For safer hunting a missile weapon was used, and although the longbow was employed it was not an amateur's weapon and the crossbow was more commonly used. It could be prepared and then discharged at will, whereas the longbow had to be drawn and shot as the quarry appeared. Many of the crossbows were beautifully decorated with inlay of horn and ivory, but they were, nevertheless, immensely powerful weapons. The bow was so strong that it could not be bent by hand, and various mechanical devices such as the goat's-foot lever, the windlass, and the cranequin had to be used to span it. The short arrows, known as bolts, had tremendous penetration. Crossbows continued to be used as a hunting weapon until well into the nineteenth century, although later ones shot stones or clay balls rather than bolts.

(*Opposite top*) sixteenth-century crossbow and cranequin. (*Bottom*) boar swords and spears had stop bars to prevent deep penetration.

Swords and daggers

It was during the sixteenth century, with the evolution of distinct civilian and military styles, that specialization began. Although firearms were the important innovation, the newest weapons did not oust established ones such as the halberd and the partizan. The head of the former was, however, slightly different from that of earlier models.

Military swords were not dissimilar to the earlier styles, with a double-edged, slightly tapered blade and a simple cross-guard, usually slightly down-drooping towards the blade. A number of extra guards in the form of rings and loops were often added to the cross-guard. For civilian wear the rapier became very popular, as did an Italian weapon known as the *cinquedea*. Many civilian swords had extremely elaborate hilts, featuring every type of decoration.

Daggers were worn by most gentlemen, and one elaborate style was named 'Holbein' after this artist's designs for daggers and sheaths. The elaborate sheath was often made to hold two small knives as well as the dagger. Other daggers were simpler and in general shape resembled miniature war swords, with slightly down-curving quillons, often with the hilts bound in wire. Another simple dagger, which had been popular since the fourteenth century, was the ballock dagger.

(*Opposite*) during the sixteenth century hilts became more complex, with an increasing number of rings and loops to protect the hand. Blades were larger, and the use of the point was emphasized more.

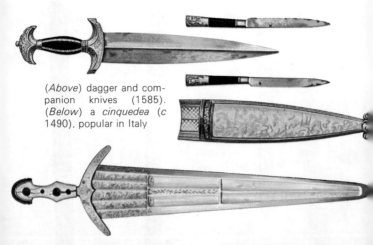

(*Above*) dagger and companion knives (1585). (*Below*) a *cinquedea* (*c* 1490), popular in Italy

Landsknechts

Swiss mercenaries with their long pikes enjoyed a period of unbroken success, and military leaders in many countries sought means to overcome their method of fighting. Emperor Maximilian I of Austria (1493-1519) recruited a body of German pikemen and halberdiers known as *Landsknechts*, and these mercenaries proved themselves ferocious and stubborn fighters. They delighted in elaborate and extravagant dress with slashing, bunches of ribbons, wide-brimmed hats, plumes, and every form of foppery, but these tastes in no way prevented them from fighting bravely.

One of their weapons was the two-handed sword standing more than five-and-a-half feet high. Blades were of two forms – either straight sided or flamboyant, with a wavy edge. Although the grip was big enough to be held in two hands, there was also a long, leather-covered ricasso, so that the blade itself could be grasped and the effective length of the weapon reduced for close-in work. Just below this ricasso there were often two lugs designed to protect the hand from an enemy blade slipping along the edge.

Members of these troops of *Landsknechts* fought with fire-arms, spears, two-handed swords, and halberds, but almost every one carried a short fighting sword in addition to the main weapon. Blades were wide and double edged, and the swords were primarily intended for slashing rather than stabbing. Grips were simple, leather covered, and widened gradually from the cross-guard to the pommel, which was usually dome shaped. Guards had a characteristic shape, with the two bars folded back into an S, often terminating with a simple knob. Many of the blades had various marks inlaid in copper, and similar marks also decorated the S-shaped guards. The scabbards were usually extremely plain and often had a pocket at the top to hold a small knife.

Landsknecht armour was very simple, with a rounded breast-plate, and leg defences reaching only to the knee. The shoulders were protected by curved lames, although many of the troops wore wide mail capes which covered the neck, shoulders, and tops of the arms. Light, open-faced helmets were worn by some, whilst others favoured a close-fitting skull-cap with a peak.

(*Above*) much favoured by the *Landsknecht* were the great two-handed swords of the sixteenth century.

(*Left*) as well as a large sword or musket the *Landsknechts* carried a sword with characteristic S-shaped quillons (*right*). They wore corselets which were usually fairly simple.

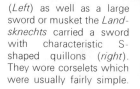

Gunpowder and guns

A weak form of gunpowder was known in China as far back as the eleventh century, but knowledge of this wonderful mixture spread only slowly. It is not known for certain when gunpowder first reached Europe, but its existence was recorded by Roger Bacon in the thirteenth century, for he gives what is usually accepted as a formula for its manufacture – a mixture of saltpetre, charcoal, and sulphur in varying proportions. This black powder burnt rapidly, produced a cloud of smoke, a loud explosion and, if used in a gun, could propel a projectile some distance.

Gunpowder in firearms seems to have occurred early in the fourteenth century, for there are references to cannon in Italy in 1326. At first its use was restricted to siege work, and it was unreliable and highly dangerous to user as well as target. Once the idea of sending a missile some distance had been established, however, it was not long before the principle was being applied to hand-guns. These new weapons were miniature cannons fastened on to the end of a stick. Both cannons and hand-guns were fired by igniting the powder by way of a small hole drilled in the barrel.

Early hand-guns were hooked over the edge of a wall and fired by means of a hot coal, wire, or ember of wood. However, this method seriously restricted the free movement of the gunner, and the introduction of the slow-burning match was a welcome improvement. The saltpetre-impregnated cord burned slowly with a glowing end and, barring accidents, would continue to burn for some time, giving the gunner freedom to move some distance from the fire.

Early firearms were crude but marked a new era in warfare: (*top*) bronze hand-gun; (*bottom*) large siege cannon.

Fourteenth-century hand-gun

Fifteenth-century matchlock

Sixteenth-century hackbut

Sixteenth-century hackbut

Sixteenth-century matchlock

German matchlock (1537)

NOT TO SCALE   Italian matchlock (*c* 1530)

In the early fifteenth century a simple, mechanical ignition system was introduced, and an S-shaped lever, the serpentine, was fixed to the side of the stock, the wooden body-frame. Pressure on the lower section swung the top one down to press the glowing end into the powder around the touch hole, so igniting the main charge to fire the gun. The shape of the wooden stock was altered to make a shoulder rest, the butt, and by the sixteenth century the musket, a hand-gun with these features, was being used by most European armies.

Gunpowder changed the whole balance of power on the battlefield. The armoured knight was no longer secure, for with little or no practice and a degree of luck the rawest recruit could kill the greatest in the land.

Armour

During the sixteenth century armours became at the same time technically outstanding and defensively inefficient. Many were decorated with superb skill, but towards the end of the century surfaces were often no longer smooth or shaped to deflect the blow quite so easily. Heavy cavalry still wore full armour with close helmets or armets. Shoulder defences were strengthened by the addition of haute pieces, plates that stood vertically from the shoulders to give extra protection to the throat. Breast-plates had a central ridge, and two fairly large tassets hung over the thighs. Foot defences no longer had pointed toes but followed the civilian style, with very broad toes. Light cavalry wore no leg armour at all and,

(*Left*) armour from Nuremberg, the burgonet being fitted with a barred visor (1540). (*Right*) Milanese armour (1510-5), still with a mail skirt

Sixteenth-century boot stirrups

unlike the heavy cavalry, their horses were completely un-armoured. Many foot soldiers wore only a light helmet and a jacket reinforced with metal plates, a brigandine or jack.

Armour was being rendered obsolete by the development of firearms. Although it was quite possible to make armour strong enough to resist a bullet, the weight became excessive, and during the second half of the sixteenth century there was a growing tendency for it to be discarded. At first only the leg defences went, but by the end of the century the only armour worn by many troops was a helmet and a breast-plate.

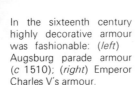

In the sixteenth century highly decorative armour was fashionable: (*left*) Augsburg parade armour (*c* 1510); (*right*) Emperor Charles V's armour.

Half armour

During the sixteenth and seventeenth centuries there was an increasing emphasis on quick movement. In place of the heavy, slow-moving cavalry of an earlier period there were quick-moving cavalry. Many wore only a corselet comprising a light helmet and a breast- and back-plate, as well as, perhaps, arm defences. Many infantry were similarly equipped. Records of the period often speak of armour known as Almain rivet, which was apparently a mass-produced half armour. Most corselets and Almain rivets comprised a collar, breast- and back-plates, tassets, an open helmet, arm defences, and gauntlets. Some lacked gauntlets but had an extension of plate over the back of the hand. To accommodate different sizes there was a sliding pin in the arm defences.

A half armour usually described as Pisan was produced in Italy, mostly in Milan. It comprised an open-faced helmet (a burgonet), a breast- and back-plate, and hung from the waist two tassets which looked like a series of lames but were

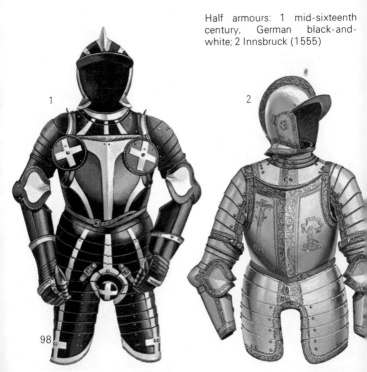

Half armours: 1 mid-sixteenth century, German black-and-white; 2 Innsbruck (1555)

made in fact from single pieces. Full arm defences were fitted, complete with elbow couters which extended round the arm. The gauntlets had wide, sweeping cuffs. This armour was frequently etched with bands of decoration. Although it looked impressive, the quality was poor, and the helmets were often not very sturdy. Some German armours comprising breast- and back-plates, helmet, and tassets were painted with black, rust-resisting paint and known as black-and-white armours.

Later examples: 1 Italian (1580-90); 2 black-and-white (*c* 1590); 3 Pisan or N. Italian (1560-70)

Parade armour

As the demand for war armour began to diminish the master armourers, no doubt, sought other outlets for their products. One profitable line was that of parade armours. Naturally, only the wealthy could afford these luxuries, for such armours were elaborate and made with little or no restriction on cost. The first manifestation of this trend can be seen in the grotesque visors which appeared about 1510. These visors – moulded into human faces, bird and animal heads – are superb examples of the armourer's skill, but their very shape defeats their prime purpose, for the projections would have held the edge of the blade rather than deflected it.

Superb technique is also illustrated in the armour made to look like civilian dress, with its metal puffing and slashing. Embossing (the hammering out of decoration into relief) was practised by Italian and German armourers, and some of the most outstanding examples of such work were the helmets produced by Filippo Negroli of Milan.

Other styles of decoration were also used to embellish the armours of the mighty. Such armours were attractive and, no doubt, created quite an impression, but rough usage must have spoilt much of the decoration. Painting was used on helmets from the thirteenth to the sixteenth century and there are references to painted body armour in the fourteenth century, but this fashion fell from favour early in the 1500s.

Etching was used until the seventeenth century; this was done by covering the surface of the metal with paint or wax and scratching the desired picture or pattern through the wax. The plate was then covered with acid and all surfaces not protected by the paint or wax were attacked. In Germany a process which was just the reverse was adopted during the sixteenth century; here the required design was painted on to the metal so that it was left untouched by the acid and stood proud from the etched surface. On some armours the etched areas were covered with a thin layer of coloured enamel, but this seems to have been a rarely-used technique.

Engraving was occasionally used, the metal being cut with a sharp, pointed tool. Gilding was done by covering the surface with a thin layer of gold, and silvering by pressing thin layers of silver foil on to roughened surfaces.

Superbly embossed helmets by Negroli of Milan (1530-40)

Finely embossed armours: made (*above*) at Innsbruck (*c* 1555) and (*right*), in the style of civilian dress, at Augsburg (*c* 1530)

To resist bullets, armour was made thicker and heavier. During the seventeenth century a type of armour composed of a fairly substantial breast-plate, long, laminated tassets reaching to the knees, and a burgonet (usually fitted with a barred visor) was worn by the heavy cavalry. It was usually described as cuirassier's armour and was largely abandoned by the middle of the century.

SEVENTEENTH CENTURY

Cuirassiers

Although the custom of wearing armour was diminishing during the sixteenth century, it was not completely discarded until late in the seventeenth century. Some heavily-armoured troops were used during the English Civil War (1642-8) and the Thirty Years War in Europe (1618-48). One type of soldier was known as a cuirassier, and he wore comparatively heavy armour. On his head he wore a close helmet, fitted with a peak and a barred visor in place of the more usual plate type; however, a number of troops still wore the conventional close helmet with full visor.

A further form of close helmet, which appeared at the turn of the century in Italy, was the type referred to as a Savoyard. It had a visor with holes pierced for eyes, nose, and mouth, and its skull-like appearance also earned it the name *Totenkopf* (death's head). Cuirassiers had mostly abandoned the use of the lance and now relied upon a good sword and a brace of pistols fitted with a new device for firing the powder, the wheel-lock. The pistols were carried in a pair of holsters at the saddle-bow.

As well as the close helmet the cuirassier wore a three-quarter armour reaching to the knees. Greaves and shoes were discarded in favour of high, leather boots. From the waist to the knees long tassets composed of many lames were worn, terminating in a poleyn and secured at the top to the lower edge of the breast-plate by straps or by turning pins which engaged with slots on the tassets. Pauldrons and vambraces (armour for the arm) were usually united into one flexible piece, with the inside of the elbow protected by small, overlapping plates; gauntlets completed the arm defences.

Breast-plates were rather flat, although many men still wore the older style, the peascod, with a central ridge terminating in a small, down-drawn point at the centre of the waist. The armour of many cuirassiers was dark, and the rivets securing the numerous lames were brass headed, lending an attractive feature to what was otherwise quite a heavy, clumsy-looking armour. Their helmets usually had rather large gorget plates which extended well down over the chest.

English Civil War armour and weapons

The seventeenth century saw the general abandonment of armour by the foot soldier; it lingered on for a while in the cavalry, where the soldiers retained their breast- and back-plates until the eighteenth century. One result of the English Civil War was the better organization of the arms trade in Britain: pressure of war revealed that the old system could not meet demand. Gunpowder made a nearly complete sweep of battlefield weapons; the matchlock musket and bayonet held sway, although the sword and, for a while, the pike were re-tained – only survivors of the armoury of staff and edged weapons. Cavalry relied on their swords and pistols, whereas the foot soldier had his musket, bayonet, and sword. For most of the Civil War the pike was given a new role in the hands of the pikeman, whose job it was to protect the musketeers

2

4

at their most vulnerable moment – when they were reloading.

Pikemen wore breast- and back-plates with wide, skirt-like tassets which looked as if they were fashioned from several lames but were, in fact, single plates made to resemble the older style. Breast- and back-plates were held in place by belts and straps which were often covered with small, overlapping, metal plates to reduce the risk of their being cut. Gloves were normally worn to protect the hands from being rubbed by the long, ash shafts of the pike. Cavalry wore somewhat similar breast- and back-plates over a thick, buff leather coat strong enough to turn aside a sword cut. To guard the vulnerable left hand, which held the bridle, a gauntlet with a cuff to the elbow was worn. A few cuirassiers served in full armour, but they were not a great success: one group of Parliamentarians was called 'a regiment of lobsters'.

Unlike musketeers (1), pikemen wore substantial armour (2), whilst cavalrymen wore a heavy cuirassier's armour (3) or a buff coat, breast- and back-plates, and bridle gauntlet (4), that shown belonged to James II.

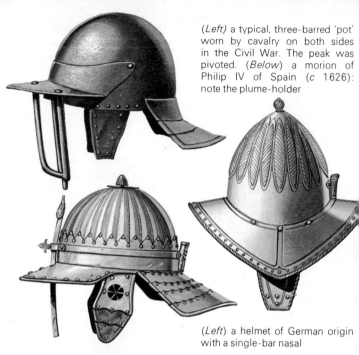

(*Left*) a typical, three-barred 'pot' worn by cavalry on both sides in the Civil War. The peak was pivoted. (*Below*) a morion of Philip IV of Spain (*c* 1626): note the plume-holder

(*Left*) a helmet of German origin with a single-bar nasal

English Civil War helmets

Possibly the most characteristic helmet of the English Civil War was the 'lobster-tail pot', worn by the cavalry of both sides. There were two varieties, which differed largely in the provisions made for face protection; those made abroad, usually in the Low Countries, had a single-bar nasal which could be raised or lowered, whereas the English variety had a three-bar arrangement attached to the pivoted peak, and this entire section could be raised or lowered. Pikemen wore either a wide-brimmed pot or a Spanish morion, also called a cabasset. All these helmets usually had earflaps which tied beneath the chin. Many had a small metal tube riveted on to the back just above the brim; this served as a plume-holder, coloured plumes being used for identification. After the middle of the sixteenth century many helmets were constructed from two pieces of metal joined together: a far easier method than fashioning them from a single piece.

Cavalrymen, especially Cavaliers, sometimes scorned a helmet and compromised by wearing a steel skull-cap beneath their usual wide-brimmed hats. The caps, secretes, were very similar to those worn under mail many centuries earlier. A few examples of steel hats copying the civilian style are known, but these were presumably made to special order for wealthier soldiers. Some very heavy and thick-walled burgonets were made, but these were intended for siege operations and were worn only for quite limited periods.

Helmets and armour of this and earlier periods were often proved, that is tested to ensure that they could stop a bullet. Most of the 'bullet' marks seen on armour are, in fact, the result of proving and not of action. Armour was described as being musket-, caliver-, or pistol-proof, indicating that it might be expected to resist these various weapons. In earlier times the proving was done with the crossbow. It was, of course, normal for the breast-plate to be much thicker than the back-plate or other pieces, and most helmets were only pistol-proof.

(*Right*) a steel helmet shaped like a civilian hat, plus an adjustable nasal. (*Below*) a German single-bar pot. Both *c* 1640

(*Right*) an Italian Savoyard helmet with the visor, which was fashioned like a face, held locked in place by a side hook (*c* 1600)

Weapons

A great variety of swords was used during this century, including several which had evolved from earlier models. The most common, certainly in Britain, was the cavalry broadsword. Fitted with blades of varying widths, sometimes two or three inches wide, it had several short fullers just below the guard. Hilts were quite elaborate, a series of bars springing from the pommel and ending below the grip to form a basket to protect the hand. Often the bars were chiselled; many had a head believed to be a death mask of Charles I cut into them and gained the swords the title of mortuary swords.

Infantry swords tended to be somewhat similar in design, with far fewer bars, but often featured a shell-guard, which was a metal plate fitting into a loop at the bottom of the grip. Many had a loop on the right side called a thumb-ring, through which the thumb was passed to ensure a good grip.

Rapiers and broadswords were the swords most generally used during the first half of the seventeenth century. Most of them had hilts which were simpler in design than previously.

As the musket and pistol developed, many older types of weapon were discarded or relegated to ceremonial duty. This is particularly true of staff weapons such as glaives, halberds, and partizans. Many were produced with highly decorative blades, often bearing the owner's coat-of-arms. Blades were also gilded and pierced, and certain features exaggerated so much that they lost any practical use. Shafts were often covered with velvet, and fringes were fitted below the heads, although some earlier, more practical, weapons were similarly treated to prevent rain or sweat making the shafts slippery.

In eastern Europe changes tended to come much later, and certain pole-arms and weapons such as the war hammer were still used after western Europe had abandoned them. The wearing of armour also lingered on here. The lance was abandoned after the English Civil War and was not revived until the eighteenth century when Napoleon incorporated some Polish lancers into his army and started a new fashion.

Cavalry picks were still used, but most pole-arms had become less practical, being mainly for ceremonial purposes and bodyguards.

Rapiers

Early sword-play was a matter of slashing, parrying, and brute strength or quick stabs with the *estoc*. War swords were often used with a two-handed grip and were known as hand-and-a-half swords. As the custom of hooking the forefinger over the cross-guard became more general, there was need to protect the finger, and loops were added to the hilt. Moreover, as armour was worn much less frequently, swords became lighter, and there was a much greater emphasis on the use of the point.

All these factors combined to produce the rapier, which probably first emerged in Spain. The term is recorded as early as 1474 and derived from *espada ropera*, a dress or costume sword. About 1550 the term was applied to a light cut-and-thrust sword used mostly by civilians, with a long, two-edged blade and a guard of bars and loops.

From about 1560 a rapier meant a light, thrusting sword for fencing, a type of sword-

As fencing increased in popularity in the late sixteenth and seventeenth centuries rapiers became very common. Hilts vary greatly in the number and arrangement of bars and guards.

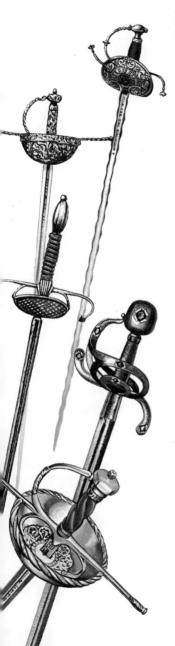

play which had developed in Italy and spread into most of Europe. Blades were, at first, very long – up to five feet – and double edged, but later they were shortened to more manageable proportions. Hilts became more complex, and by about 1570 they had acquired the style known as swept hilt. At the same time some of the lower rings were fitted with plates, often pierced, which were later enlarged to form two round shells. Swords with such hilts were called Pappenheimers after a commander in the Thirty Years War. In England the bottom rings were often replaced by two cup-like plates, often featuring inlaid silver decoration. All this culminated in the appearance of the cup-hilt rapier in the second quarter of the seventeenth century. It was popular in Italy and Spain, where it was used until well on into the eighteenth century. However, during the seventeenth century blades were becoming shorter and hilts simpler as the small-sword evolved.

During the second quarter of the seventeenth century the bars on the hilt were often replaced by a cup with long quillons. This cup-hilted rapier was especially popular in Spain and Italy.

Daggers were common wear during the seventeenth century, and some were used in the left hand as an auxiliary weapon in fencing.

Left-hand daggers

Daggers were never a prime military weapon but were carried by most soldiers and civilians for self-protection. During the sixteenth century the quillon dagger, which was more or less a miniature version of the full-sized sword, came into general use in a variety of forms, some extremely decorative, with chiselled pommels and quillons. The type first appeared in the thirteenth century and has been in use ever since.

As fencing developed the increasing emphasis on the use of the point stimulated the Masters of Fence to devise means whereby the fencer might guard himself against the point of his opponent's sword. The general aim was to parry, or knock aside, an opponent's blade. It was done with the sword blade or by an auxiliary device. Some teachers advocated the use of a mailed gauntlet to grasp the blade, others a cloak around the arm as a simple shield. However, one of the most popular aids was a dagger used, point upwards, in the left hand.

Quillon daggers were used in this way to catch and divert

the point of the rapier and, to give extra protection, a ring was mounted on the quillon block. Most of these daggers have a substantial ricasso, so that the ball of the thumb could be pressed down on the blade to ensure a firm grip. The quillons were often curved slightly downwards and forward to offer a little extra protection to the hand. Many such daggers were made *en suite*, in the same style as the companion rapier and decorated in the same fashion. Blades were usually stiff, and some earlier versions are ribbed and pierced.

Fencing with left-hand daggers enjoyed a vogue until about 1630. After this left-hand daggers were gradually discarded, except in Spain and Italy where they were popular until well into the eighteenth century. Spain developed a type with long, thin quillons and a shell-guard springing from the quillon and tapering up to the pommel. A slight depression on the broad ricasso took the ball of the thumb. The blade often had a series of notches designed to catch the opponent's blade, and a few had teeth to catch, hold, or break a blade.

Spanish left-hand daggers were distinguished by large hand-guards. Notched edges were sometimes fitted to catch or break a blade.

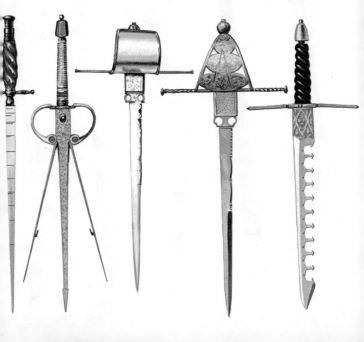

Hunting swords and hangers

Hunting retained its popularity throughout the Middle Ages and continued to be enjoyed by many of the leisured classes during the seventeenth and eighteenth centuries. All the traditional weapons, including the crossbow, were still used, but during the seventeenth century a short sword was usually carried by the hunter. Such a weapon might be referred to as a hunting sword, a hanger, or a riding sword, but the distinctions, if any, are very small. Just as travel was hazardous and some convenient sword was needed for self-defence, so in hunting a short sword was handy for dispatching wounded game: on both occasions the weapon used could be called a

These general-purpose swords were known as riding swords, hangers, or hunting swords. Many have hilts of staghorn with a side shell.

hanger. The distinguishing characteristic of this group of swords is that their blades are curved, an unusual feature as most European swords – apart from the falchion, in use from the early thirteenth century – were straight bladed.

Hangers were almost invariably simple in design and construction. In general they were short, with a blade that seldom exceeded two feet or so in length. Blades of the seventeenth century were slightly curved, single edged, and of sturdy construction. It was not uncommon for them to have some mark stamped on them; this was the trademark of the cutler. In London almost all cutlers were members of the London Cutlers' Company, and each had his own device, initials, or emblem with which all his goods were supposed to be marked.

Hilts varied in detail, but basically they consisted of a grip, usually of stag's horn, a simple knuckle-bow, and a short, down-curved back quillon. Many had a side shell which often carried a scene of hunting or mythology. There was no pommel, but simply a cap to top the horn grip and hold the end of the knuckle-bow. Guards were usually of brass, sometimes of steel; the few intricate ones were obvious exceptions. Scabbards were generally of leather, often plain but occasionally with a simple decoration of incised lines. Fittings were of brass or steel, frequently to match the knuckle-bow, and a long prong attached the weapon to the belt or sling.

Sixteenth-century falchion

Italian falchion, dated 1618

German hanger (c 1640)

English hanger (1750-1)

English, saw-backed hanger

Bayonets and stilettos

Gunpowder certainly altered the emphasis and balance of warfare and may, with justification, be described as the initiator of technological warfare. However, there were drawbacks and problems for the gunners and musketeers. Not least among these was the powder itself, which tended to be variable in quality and uncertain in performance. Gunners had to be able to calculate the amount of powder required to throw a certain size of shot a certain distance, and it was appreciated that it was not always convenient for a soldier to carry a book of tables. One solution was to use the gunner's stiletto, which served the double purpose of dagger and calculator; the sides of the triangular blade were marked off with sundry tables to assist the master gunner in his calculations. Most gunners' stilettos had a simple cross-hilt and were fashioned completely of metal, and many were of Italian origin.

For the musketeer the problems were less academic and far more serious: having fired his musket he was defenceless, with a heavy and cumbersome weapon in his hands, until he had reloaded. One solution was to guard him with groups of pikemen, but this wasted man-power, and around the middle of the seventeenth century another method was evolved whereby the useless musket could be converted into a short pike to hold off the cavalry. This conversion was simple and was achieved by pushing a knife, hilt first, into the barrel. Thus the bayonet was created, although the same name had earlier been applied to a knife made at Bayonne in France.

Obviously the bayonet imposed limitations, for with it in position it was impossible to load or fire the musket. Attempts to overcome this were soon in hand, and a fitting using lugs enabled the bayonet to be fastened on to the outside of the barrel. The most successful system, however, was that using a tubular socket which dropped over the barrel and was then held in position by a stud or, later, a spring clip. This system evolved late in the seventeenth century and was in general use by the mid-eighteenth. Late in the nineteenth century another system, using a stud on the side of the barrel and a groove on the hilt of the bayonet, became more general, and with minor modification this system has remained in use up to the present.

(*Below*) a seventeenth-century, English plug bayonet. (*Centre*) a late seventeenth-century, all-steel gunner's stiletto, its blade marked with tables used in calculating charges of powder. (*Right*) a highly decorated, Spanish plug bayonet, probably a hunting weapon (*c* 1770)

Small-swords

Rapiers were popular during the first half of the seventeenth century, but as towns became more crowded there was less room for extravagant fashions and this long-bladed weapon was gradually abandoned. New types of sword, shorter, lighter, and more convenient for town wear, were evolved. From about 1630 the length of the blade was gradually reduced, and the complex system of bars and loops in earlier hand-guards was modified. About the same time there appeared a type of rapier with two fairly large, saucer-like shells and two long quillons which curved down towards the point. Two arms sprang from the quillons and curved to meet the inside base of the shells; there was often no knuckle-bow.

By the middle of the century most blades were about thirty inches long. Quillons and the arms of the hilt were shortened, and many swords were fitted with smaller shells. Not only were the shells made smaller but they were also flattened and, at a later date, lost their raised borders. This was the basic form of the small-sword, and much decorative skill was lavished on it, with chiselling of the hilt, silver inlay, and later hilts sometimes fashioned completely of silver.

Another type of sword popular towards the end of the seventeenth century was the pillow-sword with its simple hilt of two quillons and perhaps a side ring. Dish-hilt rapiers were primarily duelling weapons with large, flat dish-guards.

Small-swords became part of gentlemen's everyday costume and were to remain so for a century, with the style basically unchanged. In the last quarter of the seventeenth

century the knuckle-bow was once again common on these swords, and the quillons were reduced still further in size. By the turn of the century the forward quillon below the knuckle-bow had largely been abandoned, whilst the rear one was debased into a short, rather bulbous termination extending only a little beyond the shells. Pommels became more egg-shaped, and the grips were generally square or oval in section, thick at the centre, and tapering towards both ends. Many grips were bound with wire, which not only looked attractive but ensured a firm hold. Blades were generally double edged and tapered to a sharp point.

In general seventeenth-century swords had simple hilts with wire-bound grips, and many had some high-relief decoration.

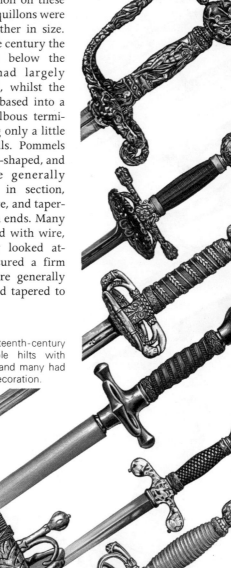

EIGHTEENTH CENTURY
Hangers

Hangers continued in fashion throughout the eighteenth century and, as a broad generalization, it may be said that they tended to become more elaborate. Some retained the curved blade, but straight blades were far more common and these were often etched. Hilts varied greatly in design, and many dating from the early part of the century have shells projecting sideways or downwards, parallel with the blade.

Knuckle-bows were retained on some swords, but others had only short quillons, sometimes with a decorative chain linking the front quillon with the cap. Grips were of wood, horn, stained ivory, or wood covered with a thin layer of tortoise-shell. A few hangers were made with a flintlock pistol fitted to the hilt and partially covered by the side shell. Sheaths were still made of leather, although the mounts were a

The majority of eighteenth-century hunting swords were fitted with straight blades and hilts of brass. Some grips were made of stag's horn, see the detail (*left*), but others had a covering of tortoise-shell.

little more elaborate, many European examples being fitted with a pocket which held a knife and fork. In Germany hunters carried hangers right up to this century.

Hunting during the seventeenth and eighteenth centuries retained its popularity, and most of those taking part carried one form or other of the typical hunting swords. However, amongst the servants of the hunt one, at least, would have carried the elaborate wood-knife, which is also known as the *trousse de chasse*. This complete kit was housed in an elaborate metal-and-leather sheath and comprised the equipment required to dispatch and dismember the kill – usually a stag or boar. The largest of the items was a broad-bladed, heavy, cleaver-like knife. Most *trousses* had a variety of more usual knives, forks, and bodkins, and these were used in cutting up the carcass. Many of the wood-knives that have survived belonged to monarchs and princes and, as befits such princely possessions, they bear the arms of the owner and are decorated with ivory, and with gilt and other precious metals.

Somewhat similar to the large cleaver were the elaborate knives called *présentoir*, used as their French name implies in the serving of food at table. They had a wide, flat blade with a handle often set in the centre of the blade.

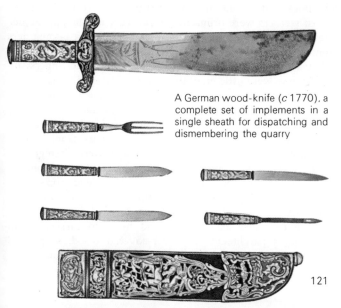

A German wood-knife (*c* 1770), a complete set of implements in a single sheath for dispatching and dismembering the quarry

Small-swords

Every man with any pretensions to quality wore a sword in town; this practice continued until about 1780 when the sword, as an article of everyday wear, was generally abandoned. Considerable sums of money were expended on these delicate but deadly weapons and, although there are numerous variations in detail, the basic style remained unaltered.

Knuckle-bows were general until the end of the period, when some of the dress swords had only a chain-guard like that on some hangers. Apart from this feature it is possible to date many examples by comparing certain features like shells, blades, and the arms of the hilt. Early seventeenth-century examples of the small-sword have two distinct shells, often with one larger than the other. However, as the century progressed the two shells were more often made the same size and then combined to form a rather flattened figure of eight which, by the 1760s, had become an oval. It is this shape that is found on the late eighteenth- and early nineteenth-century dress swords.

Another useful feature for dating the sword is the size of the loops formed by the arms of the hilt as they curve back to meet the shells. In certain styles of fencing the fingers could be hooked over the quillon and slipped into these rings. As most wearers were primarily concerned with the appearance rather than the use of the weapon, these rings became less important and were gradually reduced in size. By the 1750s they were usually too small to accommodate the fingers; by 1780 they were little more than almost flattened bars.

One variation was the boat-shell hilt; here the two shells were united into a single heart-shape with the point curving up and splitting to accommodate the forward quillon. The Heavy Cavalry dress sword for officers, worn from 1796 to 1834, was of this style. Small-sword blades were often ground hollow and in section resembled a thin triangle with concave sides. A similar type, the *colichemarde*, had a wide top section but narrowed sharply about one-third of the way down to a very narrow, thrusting point. Every form of decoration was used to embellish small-swords, and they were carried in thin sheaths of parchment or leather-covered wood, suspended from the waistband or belt by a hanger of small chains.

(*Above*) English, silver-hilted small-sword, hallmarked 1724

(*Above*) English, all-steel small-sword (*c* 1790), blued. (*Below*) English mourning sword with black-bound grip (*c* 1750)

(*Left*) French small-sword with a silver hilt (*c* 1760). (*Below*) late small-sword, with a chain replacing the solid knuckle-bow

NINETEENTH CENTURY

Armour

Armour had been abandoned in Britain for many years, but many European countries had retained it for their cavalry. Spain, France, and Prussia continued to equip some of their cavalry units with breast- and back-plates as a means of protection, although the practice was lessening and wars such as the Crimean and the American Civil War were demonstrating that armour was no longer worthwhile. It is interesting to note that the French heavy cavalry who went into battle in World War I were wearing armour and helmets that differed but little from those worn by the charging cavalry at Waterloo.

George IV, whose military interest was largely limited to uniforms, brought armour back into the British Army; he had the Household Cavalry don breast- and back-plates and, a little later, metal helmets were also adopted. Some of the helmets worn by British and foreign cavalry were highly

Some nineteenth-century armour: Danish general's helmet (*below*); British Household Cavalryman's cuirass (*right*)

decorative but totally impractical, with huge, top-heavy crests. They were, in fact, more decorative than protective, and the same applies to the Household Cavalry's armour.

Apart from the cuirass and metal helmets, which were generally limited to cavalry, the last bit of armour to survive in the British Army was the gorget. It will be remembered that originally this was worn to protect the neck, but when the main body armour was discarded during the seventeenth century some gorgets were retained and became formalized into large, decorative, crescent-shaped pieces of metal hung around the neck. During the eighteenth century they became smaller and far less decorative. Most were of gilt brass, but some were of silver; all bore some engraving. Most bore the royal cypher, and some the regimental number.

In 1796 it was ordered that all gorgets should bear the royal cypher and a wreath, and this remained the basic style until they were finally abolished in 1830. Gorgets were suspended around the neck by a length of ribbon and were worn only by officers, as a badge of rank. Elsewhere in Europe the practice of wearing gorgets continued to a much later date, and during the Third Reich the Germans revived the practice.

References in eighteenth-century military books to breast-plates do not, as a rule, mean a cuirass but the small, decorative plate worn on the cross-straps at the chest and now called a shoulder-belt plate. It was abandoned in 1855.

British officer's gorget

Bayonets

During the nineteenth century the bayonet was still regarded as a useful device, and many versions were produced. If there was any general trend it was towards an increase in the length. Many had blades up to three feet long, although this type was really an attempt to produce a sword-bayonet – a weapon which could be fitted onto the end of a barrel or used as a separate sword.

Early in the nineteenth century a rifle designed by a London gunsmith, Ezekiel Baker, was adopted by the British Army. It had a brass-hilted bayonet which engaged with a bar on the side of the barrel. This was an uncommon method of attachment; most long-arms still used a socket fitting. About the middle of the nineteenth century a stud, on the side of the barrel, which engaged with a slot in the bayonet grip became the usual method of attachment. There was a fashion for *yataghan* bayonets, with curved blades, about the same time.

As firearms became more

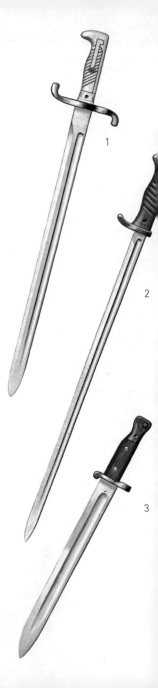

Bayonets: 1 & 2 German Mausers, patterns 1871 and 1898; 3 British Lee Metford (*c* 1890)

sophisticated, with magazines holding several cartridges, the bayonet, never a convenient weapon, became far less important. It was shorter, and the stud-and-socket fitting became more or less universal. Blades were straight, although their section was not always conventional. The Lebel had a blade with a cruciform section, and some later Enfield bayonets were rather like long bodkins.

In addition to bayonets some troops carried a short side-arm which, in the case of engineers and associated troops, often had a saw-edged back to the blade. With this the side-arm became a tool as well as a weapon. A number of rather special weapons were produced, such as the Elcho bayonet, used during the Ashanti War in 1873 to fit on the Snider rifle. It had a straight, saw-backed blade which widened about half-way along into a spear-head shape and was intended as a useful aid in clearing brush and wood. It must, however, have been rather point-heavy; in any case it was soon withdrawn from service.

Bayonets with unusual blades:
1 French Lebel (post 1916);
2 English *yataghan* (c 1860)

Uniforms and weapons

During the nineteenth century Europe's army uniforms were at their most splendid. They were a riot of colours and a profusion of gold braid, loops, spare jackets, and similar fripperies. This extravagant style had originally been set by the Imperial Army of Napoleon, and other nations followed suit by copying, improving, and embellishing its designs. There was also a tendency for countries to copy the uniforms of the victors of any war, and even in some cases those of the vanquished. However, from the middle of the century there was a gradual simplification of uniforms, and most of the extravagances were abandoned.

Helmets were worn by many units but were primarily the prerogative of the cavalry. In Britain the helmets were impressive, if impractical; the pattern of 1822 was a so-called 'Roman' style, with a skull of thin steel decorated with gilt leaves and the royal arms and surmounted by an enormous crest of bearskin. How a rider kept the helmet on and retained

Nineteenth-century uniforms, particularly cavalry ones, were a riot of colour and decoration. (*Left*) Spanish cuirassiers (*c* 1845). (*Right*) officer of the British 11th Hussars (*c* 1850)

his seat is a mystery. Russians and Prussians favoured helmets of more reasonable size but then surmounted them with large gilded or silvered eagles, horsehair plumes, or bunches of feathers.

Many cavalry units wore plain breast-plates, but others had applied decorations of stars and eagles. Cavalry swords were fairly long bladed and usually straight or, at most, slightly curved. Most hilts were basically simple, with a guard not dissimilar to the British Gothic pattern. The sword-belt was often elaborate, with stripes and decorated buckles, and hanging from the side was the sabretache, which was originally intended as a message pouch but which soon became yet another form of decoration, with embroidered and braid cyphers and regimental crests. A brace of pistols was carried by most cavalry men, in holsters slung from the saddle.

Infantry weapons were limited to musket and bayonet for the great majority of troops, although a few carried special swords or even, occasionally, pole-arms.

(*Left*) two Russian cuirassiers (*c* 1850). (*Right*) a French lancer of the Imperial Guard

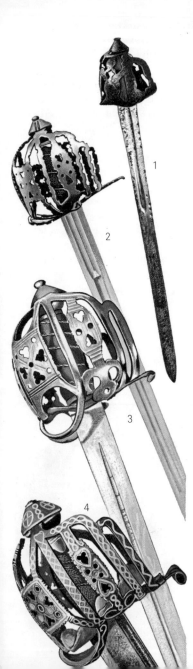

Scottish weapons

Possibly the weapon which everybody connects with Scotland is the claymore. Strictly speaking a claymore was a large, two-handed sword used by the Scots during the sixteenth and seventeenth centuries. A long, straight blade was fitted to a straight hilt, also very long, with two shortish, downsloping quillons terminating in a pierced shamrock pattern. In the seventeenth century the quillons were more curved, and a large shellplate was fitted at the side to protect the hands.

This, then, was the true 'great sword', the claymore or, in Gaelic, *claidheamh mòr*, but for the last two hundred years the term has been applied to the basket-hilted broadsword. The basket-hilt probably had its beginnings in Germany and, apart from bars, often incorporated solid plates. By the seventeenth century this full basket-hilt was in use in Scotland and has continued to be favoured there until the present. The inside of the basket is fitted with a layer of leather.

Basket-hilts: 1 late seventeenth-century; 2 eighteenth-century; 3 c 1800; 4 c 1740

Blades are straight and two edged and, in the past, often bore the name of Andrea Farrara, blade-maker, whose name was a guarantee of quality, pirated for years after his death.

The Scots were not the only troops to carry the basket-hilted broadsword, for some British dragoon regiments carried swords with a similar basket hand-guard. The Scots also carried a large dagger which became known as a dirk, although in the seventeenth century the term was used for some other weapon. The dirk probably developed from the older ballock dagger. Hilts were simple, with a flat top pommel and two lobes at the base where the blade joined the grip. The wood was often carved with typically Celtic, interwoven strap decoration. Blades were usually straight, tapering to a point; many early examples utilized cut-down sword blades.

In the nineteenth century there was a romantic revival of all things Scottish, and numbers of dirks were made, usually with a large cairngorm set in the pommel and with a sheath fitted with pockets to hold cutlery. Small daggers worn in the sock and called *skean dhu* also seem to have originated with the revival although, no doubt, some earlier knives had been carried like this. Scottish shields were round and made of wood-covered leather reinforced with brass-headed nails.

Wood-and-leather, Scottish targe

Scottish dirks developed from the earlier ballock dagger.

TWENTIETH CENTURY
World War I

The Crimean War (1854-6) could well be described as the last of the picturesque wars in which uniforms were glamorous and impractical. The American Civil War (1861-5) and the Boer War (1899-1902) demonstrated beyond doubt that modern warfare left no room for frills. Most countries discarded these extravagances, as well as armour and helmets, and at the beginning of World War I most infantry were wearing soft caps. Many German units wore the *Pickelhaube*, but being leather it gave little protection.

When fighting finally reached the terrible stalemate in the trenches doctors found that there was a disproportionate number of head wounds. The Germans saw the need for head protection, and after advice and tests they introduced a helmet which was rather similar to the sallet. Its use dramatically reduced casualties, and naturally the other combatants followed suit; by 1916-7

World War I helmets: 1 French, also World War II; 2 British; 3 German, modified in World War II; 4 German *Pickelhaube*

most troops were wearing steel helmets or 'tin hats'.

Other forms of armour were introduced from 1914-8, including a visor-like face-guard of mail for tank crews and an almost complete armour for snipers and exposed gunners. The latter was thick, heavy, and comprised a helmet reinforce and a breastplate with simple tassets.

Trench warfare saw the introduction of raiding parties which crept across no man's land to obtain information or prisoners. For the silent, vicious fighting involved, a number of fighting, or trench, knives were developed. Many were no more than cut-down bayonets or blades crudely mounted in simple hilts, but a number were commercially produced, and some could be folded away.

Despite the emphasis on the bayonet's terrors preached by militarists, the weapon was used mostly for opening tins and as a cooking implement. If it had any purpose it was for holding off cavalry, and it became obsolete as cavalry disappeared.

World War I saw much hand-to-hand combat. Besides bayonets, many forms of fighting or trench knives were used.

Nazi daggers

Solingen was always a noted centre for weapon production and as such had prospered. With Germany's defeat in World War I came financial disaster, with factories idle and craftsmen unemployed despite attempts to branch out into other fields. When the Nazis took control in 1933 some of these craftsmen and factory-owners approached Hitler, the new German leader, with the suggestion that some form of dagger would complete the uniform of his many minions by adding a decorative but war-like touch. Since it would certainly do this and also ensure the industry's financial recovery the Nazis agreed.

One of the most attractive styles selected was based on the Holbein dagger of the sixteenth century. This type was made with a bright steel blade etched or engraved with various mottoes. A hilt of wood was fitted to the blade, and its colour determined by the unit to which it was issued. Storm-troopers of the Sturm-Abteilung wore an Holbein dagger which had a brown hilt and a matching scabbard, whereas members of the Transport Corps, the NSKK, had the same dagger but with a black sheath. The dreaded élite, the SS, had a black hilt and a black scabbard. All were usually suspended by a small leather strap passing through a ring on the scabbard.

The Luftwaffe, the German Air Force, had two different versions, both having a basically cruciform hilt with flared quillons and a grip which could be any one of a number of colours. Army officers carried a dagger rather similar to those worn by the Luftwaffe, although the pommels differed and the quillons had a different centre figure. Naval daggers had the pommel in the form of an eagle.

Daggers were also issued to a wide range of officials, including those in the Fire Department, Customs, Air Raid Protection, Forestry, and even the Red Cross, although the latter carried a dagger with a saw back and a blunt point which could be used as a screwdriver. As well as the standard patterns there were more elaborate ones, which were for presentation models, with decorated blades and often more elaborate sheaths and hanging chains. The Germans also produced dress bayonets which looked like genuine bayonets but, in fact, could not be fitted to a rifle, being purely for show.

Hitler introduced the issue of dress weapons to many units. A popular style was based on the so-called Holbein dagger.

(*Above*) a Holbein dagger

(*Above*) NSKK

(*Above*) Nazi Navy
(*Below*) National Flying Corps

(*Below*) another Nazi dress weapon: a police bayonet

Differences between helmets were mostly only a matter of detail.

World War II

World War II saw an enormous increase in the use of armour in all forms, with many styles incorporating new materials. Steel helmets were still worn and were basically the same as those worn in World War I. The German helmet differed slightly in that the brim was not as deep as the 1916 pattern, but otherwise it was essentially the same. Special patterns were produced for parachute troops; these usually had no brim and were fitted with a double chinstrap.

Bayonets were still carried by most troops, although they were probably used even less than in World War I. The new British bayonets were far shorter, but naturally many older models from stock were still issued. Body armour was used, again only on an extremely limited scale. Bullet-proof waistcoats were made using a form of scale armour, although here the metal plates dropped into the pockets of an overgarment and were fashioned of new metals. Armour plate was fitted to

A British Cromwell
tank, 75 mm gun

World War II helmets: 1 American; 2 Russian; 3 Italian; 4 Japanese

aircraft to offer aircrew some protection against fighters' bullets or splinters from anti-aircraft shells.

Caterpillar tracks were not a new idea and armour was many thousands of years old, but it was not until 1916 that the two ideas were combined to produce the tank. The new invention was never fully exploited in World War I, but between the wars theories of tank warfare were developed, as the Germans demonstrated in 1940, when their Panzer units outflanked and broke the Allied lines. Armour had to be thickened as new guns were introduced, and this greater weight called for more powerful engines and more careful design to present as small a target as possible, while offering a good glancing surface. The Allies used the Sherman tank most; it came into general service in 1941. On the German side the Panther and Tiger tanks proved to be extremely versatile and tough vehicles. Variations of the tank were numerous and included flame throwers, bridge builders, and mine exploders.

An American tank, the Pershing

BRITISH MILITARY SWORDS FROM 1600

The seventeenth century saw the beginning of uniformity in the design of military swords, but still nothing emerged that could really be called a regulation pattern. However, certain types were associated with special groups of soldiers, and one of the most spectacular was the *schiavona*, used by the Schiavoni, a group of Balkan mercenaries who served the republic of Venice. This was a broadsword, with a distinctive hilt in the shape of an elaborate basket which varied in detail but basically was made up of a number of wide, often engraved, bars. Pommels were of an unusual shield-shape with an embossed centre decoration, often a lion's head.

Many privately purchased military swords were engraved or etched with the cutler's name and often his address as well. Off-duty officers frequently wore a type of sword known as a spadroon; this was very simple, with a straight, double-edged blade and a plain, curved knuckle-bow.

1 & 3 *schiavonas*, late seventeenth century; 2 Dragoon's sword, early eighteenth century; 4 spadroon, late eighteenth century

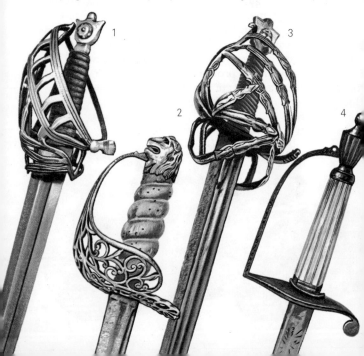

Scabbards were of leather or, more rarely, wood covered with leather, until the appearance of the 1796 pattern sword for the Light Dragoons with its steel scabbard. Most scabbards were suspended from a waist- or shoulder-belt by means of a hook on the sheath or by straps clipped on to rings on the scabbard. Since swords were purchased en bloc from different suppliers, it is quite possible to find that examples of the same pattern sword differ in detail. Many blades were imported from Germany and then mounted in Britain. As a symbol of rank British army sergeants in the infantry carried a halberd, until the practice was abolished in 1792.

Naval swords were even less standardized than army swords, although a spadroon-type weapon with a carved, five-ball motif on the knuckle-bow was quite common. When the shell-guard was introduced the part on the right-hand side of the hilt, nearest the wearer, could be folded down to let the weapon hang straight. Many had a stud at the top of the scabbard to secure the sword and prevent loss.

1 Infantry sword, and 2 officer's small-sword, both mid-eighteenth century; 3 & 4 cavalry swords, late eighteenth century

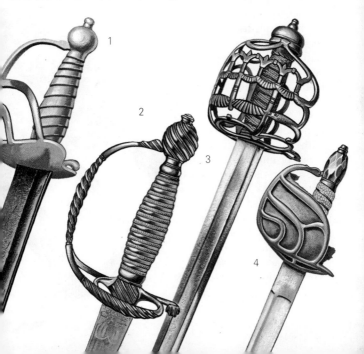

British infantry in the eighteenth century carried swords as well as bayonets, the two being suspended from a cross-belt, but it was found that most infantry had little use for their swords, and so it was decided to retain the bayonet only. In 1768 an official order abolished the infantry sword except for officers and for Scottish troops, who retained their broadswords. Swords of infantry officers were, as a rule, straight bladed, although some were curved. They had to conform to regulations, but as they were purchased privately by the officers there were often minor variations.

There was a great vogue for decorated blades among officers during the eighteenth century, blueing and gilding being especially popular. Blades were also frequently engraved or etched with the royal cypher, military patterns, and mottoes, less often with the regimental badge, name, or number. Many bore the maker's name. Obviously it would have been disastrous to lose a sword in battle, and consequently most of them had a sword-knot, a leather loop which could be slipped over the wrist as a safeguard. The sword-knot was secured to the sword by looping it through a slot or ring on the hilt.

At the end of the eighteenth century most infantry officers carried the sword usually described as the 'pattern of 1796', with its straight, narrow blade, simple, twin shells, knuckle-bow, and a pommel shaped like a classical urn. A new order of 1803 introduced a curved, wider blade and a far more elaborate cast knuckle-bow which, in the case of ordinary infantry officers, incorporated the royal cypher; for officers of the Light Company there was a bugle horn below the cypher. This pattern lasted until 1822 when the so-called Gothic hilt was introduced; this had a knuckle-bow from which other bars sprang out to sweep round and form a simple hand-guard incorporating a circle which held the royal cypher. The blade was slightly curved and had a pipeback, a thickening running along the back edge. The basic pattern of the hilt remained unchanged until 1892 when, in place of the looped, Gothic hilt, a simpler one of sheet steel was introduced.

The shape of cavalry swords was very much a matter of function; thus the light cavalry troopers carried a fairly light sword with a curved blade and a stirrup hilt. This pattern, introduced in 1796, continued in use until the 1820s. The sword was carried in a steel scabbard with two carrying rings mounted on the back.

(*Opposite*) hilt details of: 1 1831 pattern; 2 broadsword (*c* 1850); 3 1796 pattern; 4 & 5 swords of flank officer (*c* 1810) and heavy cavalry officer (*c* 1800). (*Below*) swords: 1 1803 pattern, infantry officer; 2 1827 pattern, naval officer; 3 bandsman (*c* 1850)

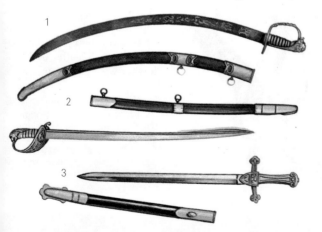

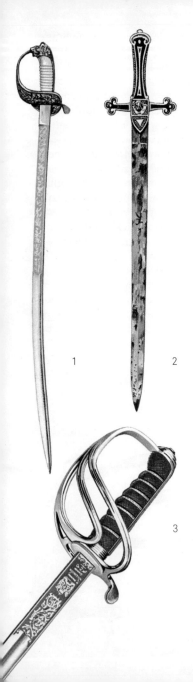

Infantry officers' swords remained straight, and in 1892 the guard still carried on ceremonial occasions by British Army officers was introduced. It was steel, decorated with a pattern of scrolls and loops which incorporated the royal cypher. With its rather sharp edge the guard was uncomfortable to carry on the belt, and in 1895 the inside edge was curved to reduce this discomfort.

A new pattern sword for general officers was introduced in 1831. Tradition has it that the style was based on a sword the Duke of Wellington brought back from India; certainly the hilt resembled that of the Persian and Turkish *shamshir*, a curved sword. The blade was slightly curved and was fitted with a simple cross-guard, each quillon terminating with a small knob. The grip was straight, with a sharp, forward curve at the top and a hole piercing this section to take the sword-knot loop. Sheaths of black leather with gilt mounts were

(*Left*) 1 a German Imperial Navy sword; 2 a mid-nineteenth century band sword; 3 the Gothic hilt. (*Opposite*) 1908 cavalry sword: 1 hilt detail, showing the well-designed grip; 2 engraved bowl on the officer's model.

used for formal occasions, but for service wear the scabbard was much more serviceable, being made of brass.

Special bodies of troops did not carry standard-issue swords, those of bandsmen were far more decorative. Hilts were often of brass, but sword designs varied from regiment to regiment, some regiments producing their own modified patterns more by custom than right.

Apart from the Japanese officers who used their swords in World War II, swords have long ceased to be serious weapons of war; certainly most infantry officers discarded theirs as so much useless lumber as soon as there was any action.

Although the cavalry had long been considered an army's main striking force and had played a dominant part in many battles, the introduction of firearms helped to render it obsolete. It lingered on until the 1914-18 War but was really out of date by the late nineteenth century. There were continual discussions about its role and about its weaponry. Lancer regiments were introduced after Waterloo, but the majority felt that the sword should remain the cavalry's main weapon. There were arguments, however, whether the sword should be used for slashing or thrusting. The verdict was in favour of a thrusting sword with a long, stiff blade. Known as the 1908 pattern, the new sword had a yard-long blade, a full bowl for the guard and, most important of all, a well-designed grip that was comfortable and shaped to bring the sword when grasped automatically to the 'charge' position. The scabbard was of steel and suspended by two rings at the top. Unfortunately the sword was 300 years too late for effective service!

AFRICA

Africa has a wealth of weapon styles, ranging from elaborately decorated daggers to crude slashing weapons. Metal was scarce for many of the inland tribes, who pressed any odd pieces into service to produce often quite elaborate daggers or short swords. Spear-heads were made in an amazing variety of shapes and sizes. Easily recognized is the long-bladed spear used by the Masai of Kenya – only a very short, wooden shaft joins the head and a very long ferrule. Further north many Somali and Sudanese spears have large, leaf-shaped heads.

Daggers from the east have a characteristic hilt, shaped rather like a double-ended T, and a blade which sweeps round almost at a right angle. Clubs do not seem to have played a great part in African warfare, apart from the *knobkerry* of the Zulu, who also used a short, stabbing spear and an oval, oxhide shield.

Swords were carried by the tribes of the Sudan and the

Oddly shaped blades of Sudanese and Congolese daggers contrast with simple cruciform swords from the Sudan and the Sahara.

Sahara, and most had long, straight, double-edged blades. Many of these were imported from Germany, but a few were old European sword blades remounted. There is, however, no foundation for the belief that these swords were left behind by the Crusaders. Possibly the legend grew up because the simple, cruciform hilt somewhat resembles the early mediaeval hilts. But there the resemblance ends, for Sudanese swords have leather-covered grips with a flat, leather disc in place of a pommel. Many have long inscriptions carved into the blade; these are most often passages from the Koran.

From Abyssinia came great, curving, sickle-like swords, *shotels,* with plain horn grips. Arabs of North Africa and the Middle East wore a dagger with an acutely-angled blade and a strengthening central ridge. Called *jambiyahs*, these are often decorated with silver wire and plates and semi-precious stones, as are the belts to which the scabbards are attached.

Top) still popular in the Middle East, the *jambiyah* or curved dagger with scabbard and belt. *Right)* African spears

AMERICA

Possibly the most famous of all American knives is the Bowie, named after a southerner, James Bowie, but mostly made in England. Its exact definition is disputed, but briefly it can be said to have a simple cross-guard, often with terminal knobs, and a broad blade with a curved section cut from the back and then sharpened to give a false edge. Sizes varied enormously, and hilts were of bone or silver, some inlaid with mother-of-pearl. Many blades were etched with patriotic mottoes and claims to Liberty and Death.

American Indians were producing flint weapons until well into the nineteenth century. They abandoned their flint knives in favour of the invaders' knives of metal, apparently trading for a broad blade which they fitted with a hilt they made themselves or else making knives, often very crudely, from any metal objects they happened to acquire. Sheaths were frequently decorated with intricate bead-work. As iron was too precious to lose, flint was still used for arrow-heads.

A number of the weapons used in America during the greater part of the nineteenth century

The tomahawk was used by most tribes. Originally deriving from an Indian word for a cutting tool, the name came to apply only to metal hatchets. An extremely popular variety was the axe-cum-pipe which dates from the late seventeenth or early eighteenth century. A small bowl at the back of the head connected with a hole drilled through the shaft. Another article of trade, it was often manufactured in Great Britain. Less well known was the tomahawk with a head like a spear, with two side arms curling back. Swords do not seem to have appealed to the Indian, but he used the lance, both as a thrusting and throwing weapon.

American swords dating from the War of Independence are many and show signs of French and English influence, the former predominating. Some features, such as the large arms of the hilt, were retained much longer than in Europe. It is not surprising that the eagle's head is a predominant motif on the pommels and quillons of many American swords.

Designs of American sword-hilts did not differ greatly from equivalent European styles.

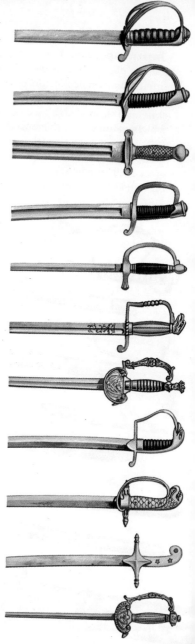

ASIA

Japanese swords

Swords of Japan have always been highly prized and are considered by many collectors to be among the finest in the world. Japanese metal workers achieved an extremely high degree of skill and knowledge and succeeded in producing blades which combined all the most desirable features, for they were stiff without being brittle and had an extremely hard edge. Manufacture was a long and complicated process requiring great skill in hammering, shaping, and quenching. After the blade had been shaped and tempered it still required hours of

(a)

polishing, and the resulting mirror-finish on many swords is still as good as ever after five centuries. Many blade-makers signed and dated their products on the tang.

The Japanese warrior or *samurai* used several sizes of swords, all basically the same in shape and general appearance. Blades were normally slightly curved and fitted with a wooden grip which was usually covered with fish skin and an intricate braid lacing. Beneath this lacing were two tiny ornaments of metal, *menuki*. Guards, *tsuba*, were almost always rectangular or circular. These flat metal plates were decorated with skill and delicacy: they were sometimes pierced with patterns or else chiselled and overlaid with precious metals.

Scabbards were generally of heavily lacquered wood and those of shorter swords had two slots, to hold a small knife, the *kodzuka*, and a skewer-like implement, the *kogai*, for arranging the hair. Swords were venerated, but in 1876 the Emperor forbad the wearing of them and, as demand stopped, the craft nearly died out. During World War II swords of the traditional pattern were mass produced, but some officers had family blades mounted in regulation fittings and carried them into action.

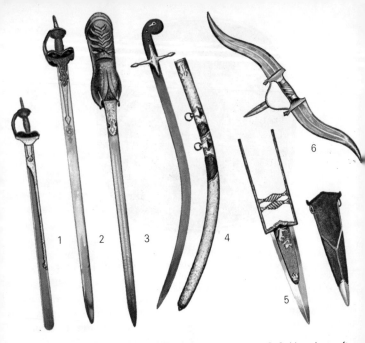

A few of the great variety of Indian weapons: 1 & 2 *khandars,* often used in two hands; 3 a *pata* or gauntlet sword; 4 a *shamshir,* 5 a *katar;* 6 a complex parrying and thrusting knife

Indian weapons

Indian edged weapons were always far more varied in design than those of Europe and, in such an enormous area as the sub-continent, this is hardly surprising. Some appear to be over-elaborate and impractical but, as most have a long history behind them, they must have proved their worth in battle.

Whereas certain parts of India tended to produce weapons peculiar to one district, the *talwar* was a sword found over a great part of the continent. It was generally, but not invariably, curved to a greater or lesser degree and had a flat disc pommel and simple cross-guard, occasionally connected by a knuckle-guard. Some *talwars* were fashioned completely of steel, but gold and silver inlay were commonly used. An unusual sword was the gauntlet sword or *pata,* which was held by slipping the hand and forearm into a gauntlet and gripping a bar. The *pata* was used largely as a lance. Scabbards were made of wood covered with various coloured materials.

For really hefty swings the Indian warrior used a *khandar*, which was a straight-bladed sword with a reinforced blade and an extension to the pommel in the form of a bar that enabled him to take a two-handed grip on the hilt. Maces were also popular with martial India; some had a spiked ball on a shaft, the end of which unscrewed to reveal a bodkin-like dagger. Flange-maces were sometimes fitted to a shaft which had a grip like that of a *khandar* sword. Daggers were produced all over India, and many of them were first-rate works of art; probably the finest were those with jade hilts. The jade was carved into animal heads, and precious stones were occasionally inserted for the eyes. Blades tended to be curved, although the *peshkabz* was normally straight bladed, with a strengthening rib at the back edge.

Peculiar to India was the *katar* or punch dagger, a miniature version of the *pata*. *Katars* had a hilt with two bars which were gripped in the fist, and the blow was delivered like a punch. Axes were less common, but some superbly decorated examples were made. Occasionally European swords were decorated in gold with typical Indian inlay work. Indian soldiers often wore armour and, although mail was retained until quite late, some plates were also used for reinforcing.

(*Left*) seventeenth-century axe of outstanding quality, decorated with gold and rubies. (*Below*) European weapons, such as this small-sword, were often decorated in 'oriental' style.

Among the least attractive weapons of India were the devices of secret and stealthy attack, and one of the most unpleasant was the tiger-claws. This vicious instrument had a number of curved steel claws fixed to a steel bar fitted with two rings, through which the first and fourth fingers slipped. It was used to give a terrible, multiple slashing wound, usually delivered with an upward sweep of the hand.

Eastern armour

Armour in the Orient developed on differing lines from that in Europe, and there was more emphasis on mail and mail combined with plate. Helmets were not dissimilar in some aspects from their European counterparts: many Indian and Turkish examples have sliding nasals like those used on burgonets of the seventeenth century. Indian and Turkish body armour was usually of mail reinforced by plates, which were frequently highly decorated with inlay. Chanfrons and horse armour of quilted fabric were worn, although most seem to have been composed of small plates with interspaced mail. Occasionally elephant armours were used. Shields were often used, particularly in India and her neighbours.

Elephant armour, possibly from the Battle of Plassey (1757)

Japanese armour was always of outstanding technical quality, and the warrior caste and frequent wars ensured its development and improvement. Most armours were composed of large numbers of lacquered metal plates laced together – lamellar armour. Helmets were fitted with very wide neck-guards, and the face was protected by a metal mask. Japanese smiths sometimes copied European styles, but on the whole Japanese armour retained its individuality.

Although Indian and Japanese arms and armour were of very good quality, those of China were almost always poor. Swords had inferior blades, and design, as in the two-handed executioner's sword, was almost crude. One exception is the pairs of swords decorated with brass and tortoise-shell.

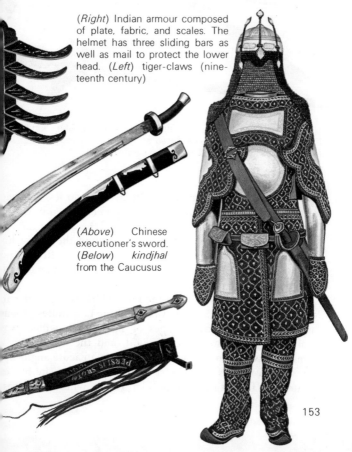

(*Right*) Indian armour composed of plate, fabric, and scales. The helmet has three sliding bars as well as mail to protect the lower head. (*Left*) tiger-claws (nineteenth century)

(*Above*) Chinese executioner's sword. (*Below*) *kindjhal* from the Caucusus

Unusual weapons: 1 a *chakram*, the steel quoit of the Sikh; 2 an Indian horn dagger; 3 a giant *talwar*, used as sacrificial weapon; 4 & 5 *kris* from Indonesia, the second with a rare kingfisher hilt

ODDITIES

Some weapons do not easily fall into neat categories, and one such is the *chakram*, which was a weapon of the Sikh. It was a flat, steel ring with a sharpened edge, and the warrior carried six of these quoits around his arm or around the top of his conical turban. It was said that, spun around the finger and then released, the revolving ring could strike down an enemy at eighty paces.

From south-east Asia came the *kris*, which was popular in Malaya, Bali, Java, and other islands of the East Indies. It was fashioned in two basic shapes of blade: one which was straight, tapering to an acute point, and the other with a number of waves in it. The grip was set at an acute angle and the weapon was used to thrust rather than slash. The blades are unusual in that the surface is left rough, whereas on most other weapons it is treated and decorated in a variety of ways. A few of the weapons were ceremonial or votive rather than warlike and had extra large, decorated blades.

Feeling the more blades the better, some sword-makers fashioned weapons with two or three blades. *Katars* were sometimes so made that, as the two holding bars of the hilt were squeezed together, the blades opened out into a trident-like weapon. Less obvious is the purpose of the two-bladed dagger here illustrated, which was carried in a double sheath. As the blades are narrow and close together its advantages are obscure. This dagger appears to be of Middle Eastern origin.

Another development was the dual-purpose weapon, such as the parrying shield of India, which had a small, round shield fitted with two iron-tipped horns so that not only could blows be parried but they could also be given. The scissors dagger was another dual-purpose weapon; it was literally a pair of scissors that could, when closed, be used as an effective stabbing weapon. Many of these appear to be of Spanish or Middle Eastern manufacture. Some daggers were disguised, like the Japanese war fan which looks like a closed fan but is, in fact, a sheath and dagger.

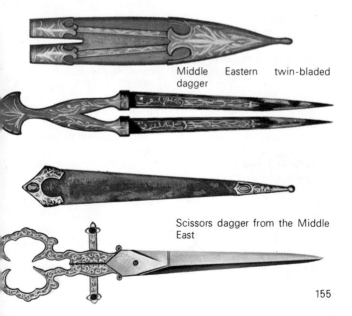

Middle Eastern twin-bladed dagger

Scissors dagger from the Middle East

GLOSSARY

Armet: 15c helmet fitted with visor and cheek-pieces at skull.

Ballock dagger: 14c-17c dagger with two lobes at grip base.

Bodkin: skewer-like piece of cutlery used in skinning and preparing of game.

Buckler: small, round shield used in sword-play – often fitted with central spike.

Burgonet: 16c-17c, light, open-faced helmet with peak and cheek-pieces.

Cabasset: 16c helmet with pointed skull and flat, narrow brim.

Caliver: light musket.

Chausses: leg defences of mail, common from the mid 12c.

Cinquedea: Italian sword with short, acutely tapered blade, popular in late 15c and early 16c. Traditionally five fingers wide at top.

Claymore: 16c-17c two-handed Highland sword. Later, name of Scottish broadsword.

Cranequin: 15c geared device for spanning or winding back string of crossbow.

Cross-guard: attachment at base of sword- or dagger-hilt, designed to protect hand.

Cuirassier: heavily armoured cavalry of 17c, armed with pistols and sword.

Estoc: 16c sword with strong, narrow blade designed for stabbing.

Ferrule: metal shoe fitted at end of lance or pike staff.

Garniture: group of armours decorated *en suite*, comprising field, tilt, and occasionally horse armour.

Goat's foot lever: simple but ingenious arrangement of levers to span crossbow of medium power.

Hauberk: long-sleeved coat of mail usually reaching to knees.

Knobkerry: club with long, thin shaft and rounded head, used by Zulus.

Lames: metal strips forming part of flexible armour.

Matchlock: system of ignition for firearms, using slow-burning match.

Partizan: long-bladed spear with short, twin, curved lugs at base.

Pauldron: shoulder defence made flexible with lames – left often slightly larger than right.

Pillow sword: light, small, rapier-like sword with single hilt – supposed to have stood by bed.

Pot: popular name for simple, wide-brimmed helmet worn by 17c pikemen.

Rondel: round plate fitted at the back of an armet.

Spanish morion: *see* cabasset.

Windlass: capstan-like device for spanning crossbow, worked by ropes and pulleys.

BOOKS TO READ

The Archaeology of Weapons by R. E. Oakeshott. Lutterworth Press, London, 1960.

The Armourer and His Craft by C. J. ffoulkes. Benjamin Blom, New York reprint 1967.

Arms and Armour by H. L. Blackmore. Studio Vista, London, 1965.

Arms and Armour by A. V. B. Norman. Weidenfeld & Nicolson, London, 1964.

Arms and Armour of the Greeks by A. M. Snodgrass. Thames & Hudson, London, 1967.

The Art of Warfare in Biblical Lands by Y. Yadin. Weidenfeld & Nicolson, London, 1963.

The Arts of the Japanese Sword by B. W. Robinson. Faber & Faber, London, 1961.

Cut and Thrust Weapons by E. Wagner. Spring Books, London, 1967.

Edged Weapons by F. Wilkinson. Guinness, London, 1970.

European and American Arms 110-1850 by C. Blair. Batsford, London, 1962.

European Armour 1066-circa 1700 by C. Blair. Batsford, London, 1958.

European Armour in the Tower of London by R. Dufty. Her Majesty's Stationery Office, London, 1968.

A Glossary on the Construction, Decoration and Use of Arms and Armour by G. C. Stone. Heffer, Cambridge, latest reprint 1969.

A History of the Weapons of the American Revolution by G. C. Neumann. Harper & Row, New York, 1967.

Indian and Oriental Armour by Lord Egerton of Tatton. Arms and Armour Press, London, new edition 1968.

Japanese Armour by L. J. Anderson. Arms and Armour Press, London, 1969.

Let's Look at Arms and Armour by F. Wilkinson. Frederick Muller, London, 1968.

Oriental Armour by H. R. Robinson. Herbert Jenkins, London, 1967.

The Small-sword in England by S. D. Aylward. Hutchinson, London, revised edition 1960.

Sword, Lance and Bayonet by C. J. ffoulkes and E. C. Hopkinson. Arms and Armour Press, London, reprint 1967.

Swords and Daggers by F. Wilkinson. Ward Lock, London, 1967.

Wallace Collection Catalogues: European Arms and Armour by Sir J. Mann. Published in London by the Trustees, 1962.

Warrior to Soldier 449-1660 by A. V. B. Norman and D. Pottinger. Weidenfeld & Nicolson, London, 1966.

INDEX

Page numbers in bold type refer to illustrations

African weapons 144-145
Aketon 57, **58**
American weapons 146-147, **146, 147**
Armet 60, 62-63, **62, 63**, 82
Armour, ancient 11, **11**, 12, **13**, 15, 17, 18-19, **19**, 20, 22
  European 16th-century 84-87, 96-101, **96, 97, 98, 99, 101**
  European 17th-century 102-105, **102, 104, 105**, 107
  mediaeval 46-48, **49**, 56-59, **56, 57, 58, 59**, 64-67, **65, 66, 67**
  modern 124-125, 133, 136-137
  Norman **30**, 31, **31**
  oriental 151, 152, 153, **153**
  Saxon 24, **24**
  Viking 28, 40
Arrow 4, **5**, 5, 7, 10, 52, **53**, 80, 88
Aventail 48, 54, 55
Axe 7, **7**, 8, **8**, 9, 25, **25**, 29, 44, 52, **53**, 79, 147, 151, **151**

Ballock dagger 90, 131
Barbuta 60
Bard 73
Bascinet 54, **54**, 55, **55**, **60**, 61, **61**, 62
Bayonet 104, 116, 117, **117**, 126-127, **126, 127**, 129, 133, 134, **135**, 136
Bevor 61, 66, 83
Bill 52, **53**, 80
Black-and-white armour **98**, 99, **99**
Bow 4, 7, 10, 30, 52
Bowie knife 146, **146**
Breast-plate 56, 57, 64, 66, 96, 103, 105, 125, 129, 133
Brigandine 97
Broadsword 108, **108**, 130-131, 138, 140, **140**
Buckler 50
Bullet-proof waistcoat 19, 136

Burgonet **96**, 98, **102**, 107
Byrnie 28, 40

Cabasset 106, **106**
Chakram 154, **154**
Chanfron 72, 73, **74**, 152
Chape 34
Chariot 6, 10-11, **10**, **11**
Chausses 46
Chinese swords 153, **153**
Cinquedea 90, **90**
Claymore 130
Close helmet 82-84, **82, 83**, 103
Club 4, 52
Coif 40, 47, **49**, 54
Colichemarde 122
Corselet 15, 17, **17**, 93, 98
Corseque 78
Couters 46, 64, 66, 99
Cranequin 88, **89**
Crinet 73, **74**
Crossbow **30**, 52, 53, 80, 88, **89**
Cuirassier 102, **102**, 103, **104**, 128, **129**
Cuir-bouilli 47, 48
Cuirie 48

Dagger **6**, 8, **8**, 45, 50, 76, **76**, 90, **90**, 112-113, **112, 113**, 131, **131**, 134, **135**, 144, **144, 145, 148**, 151, **154**, 155, **155**
Dirk 131, **131**

Egyptian weapons 6, 7, 8, **8**, 9, **9**, 10, **10**, 11
Elephant armour 152, **152**
Estoc 110

Face-guard 42-43, 133
Falchion 45, **45**, 115, **115**
Fauld 64
Fencing 110-111, 112-113
Firearms 90, 94-95, **94, 95**, 104, 116, 120, 129
Flint weapons 4, 5, **5**, 7, 146

Gambeson 47
Garniture 87
Gauntlets 47, 56, **57**, 64,

66, **67**, 85, 99, 103, 105
Gestech **70**, 71, **71**
Gladiator 23, **23**
Glaive 79, **80**, 109
Goat's foot lever 88
Gorget 47, **62**, 63, 84, 103, 125, **125**
Gothic armour 66, **67**, 85
Greaves 15, 17, **17**, 85
Greek arms and armour 12-17, **12, 13, 14**, 15, **16**, **17**
Greenwich armours 86, 87, **86, 87**
Guard chain 50, 57

Halberd **78**, 79, **79, 80**, 90, 109, 139
Half armour 98-99, **99**
Hand-axe 4, 5, **5**
Hand-guard 16, 22, 34, 76, **79**, **113**, 115
Hanger 114-115, **114, 115**, 120, 121
Haubergeon 47
Hauberk **30**, 40, 47, 56
Haute piece 96
Helm, great **43**, **47**, 48, **49**, 54, **54**, 60, 71
Helmets, ancient 12, **13**, 14, **14**, 15, **15**, 16, 17, 18, **18**, 20, 21, **21**, 22, 23
  European 16th-century 82-84, **82, 83**, 85, 100
  European 17th-century 103, 106, **106**, 107, **107**
  mediaeval 48, 54-55, **54, 55**, 58, 60-63, **60, 61, 62, 63**
  modern 124-125, **124**, 128-129, 132-133, **132**, 136, **136**, 137
  Norman 31, 42, **42**, 43
  oriental 152, 153, **153**
  Saxon 24, **24**
  Viking 28, **28**
Heraldry 37-39, **37, 38, 39**, 48, 49, 58-59
Holbein dagger 90, 134, **135**
Horse armour 48, 72-73, **72, 73**, 152
Hunting 88, 114, 121
Hunting sword 114, **114**, 120, **120**, 121

Indian weapons 150-152, 154

Jambiyah 145, **145**
Japanese arms and armour 148-149, **148**, **149**, 153
Joust **69**, 70-71

Katar 151, 155
Kettle hat 43, **43**, 47, **49**, 54, 61, 82
Khandar **150**, 151
Khopesh 9
Kindjhal **153**
Knight 48, 51, 58-59, 68-71, 75
Knobkerry 144
Kodzuka 149
Kogai 149
Kopis 16-17, **17**
Kris 154, **154**
Kukri 16

Lames 57, 92
Lance 52, 68, 71, 78, 109, 147
Landsknechts 92, **93**
Lobster-tail pot 106
Longbow 52, **53**, 80, 88

Mace 6, **6**, 7, 52, **53**, **80**, 81, 151
Mail armour 11, 20, 22, 24, 28, 31, 40-41, **40**, **41**, **46**, 49, **49**, **58**, **59**, 64, 152, 153, **153**
Maximilian armour 84-85, **84**, **85**
Mortuary sword 108
Mourning sword **123**
Mufflers 40

Nazi daggers 134, **135**
Neck-guard 42, **42**, 153
Norman arms and armour 30-36, 42-43, 88

Pappenheimer 111
Partizan 90, 109
Pata 150, **150**
Pauldron 64
Peascod 103
Peshkabz 151
Peytral 72
Pickelhaube 132, **132**
Pike 78, 104
Pillow-sword 118
Pizaine 56

Plate armour 46-47, **46**, 49, 56, 58, **58**, **59**
Pole-arms 79, **79**, 109, **109**, 129
Poleyn 46, 57, 64, 103
Présentoir 121

Quillon dagger 112-113
Quintain 68, **68**

Rapier 90, **108**, 110, **110**, 111, **111**, 118
Riding sword 114, **114**
Romans 18, 19, 20, **21**, 23, **23**, 72, 75
Rondel 63, 66, 81
Rondel dagger 76, **76**

Sallet 61, 66, **67**
Samurai 149
Savoyard 103, **107**
Saxon arms and armour 24-25, **24**, **25**
Scabbard 34, 48, 92, 115, 139, 141, 143, **145**, 149, 151
Scale armour 18-19, 20, 41, **41**, 46, **46**
Scharfrennen **70**, 71, **71**
Schiavona 138, **138**
Scissors dagger 155, **155**
Scottish weapons 130-131, **130**, **131**
Seax 25, 29, **29**
Secrete 107
Shamshir 142, **150**
Sheath 16, 90, 120-121, 122, 142
Shields, ancient 6, 9, **9**, 11, **11**, 12, **12**, 17, **17**, 20, 21, **21**, 22, 23
heraldic 38-39, **38**, **39**
Indian 155
Norman 31, 36
Saxon 24, 25, **25**
Scottish 131, **131**
Viking 27
Zulu 144
Shotel 145
Shoulder-belt plate 125
Side-arm 127
Skean dhu 131
Small-sword 11, 118, 122, **123**
Spadroon 138
Spanish morion 106, **106**
Spaulder 66
Spear **11**, 13, 19, 20, 21, **21**, 25, 29, 88, 144, **145**

Stiletto, gunner's 116, 117, **117**
Sumerian arms and armour 6, **9**
Surcoat 48, **49**
Swiss mercenaries 78, 92
Swords, African 144-145, **144**
American 147, **147**
ancient 9, **9**, 12, 13, **13**, 16, 17, 19, 20, 21, **21**, 22
European 16th-century 90, **91**, 92, **93**, 115, 130
European 17th-century 108, 110-111, **110**, **111**, 114-115, **114**, **115**, 118-119, **118**, **119**, 130, 138, **138**
European 18th-century **115**, 120-123, **138**, 139-141, **139**
mediaeval 44-45, **44**, **45**
Norman 34, **35**
oriental 148-149, **148**, 150-151, **150**, **151**, 153 **153**
Saxon 25, **25**
Viking 28, **29**
Sword-bayonet 126
Sword-belt **48**, 59, 76, 129

Talwar 150, **154**
Tank **136**, 137, **137**
Tasset 64, 96, 98-99, **102**, 103, 105, 133
Tiger-claws 152, **153**
Tomahawk 147
Tournament 69, 70
Trapper 72
Trench knife 133, **133**
Tsuba 149, **149**

Uniform 128-129, **128**, **129**

Vamplate 70, 71, 78
Viking arms and armour **26**, 27-29, **28**, **29**

War hammer 81, **81**, 109, **109**
Windlass **53**, 88
Wood-knife 121, **121**
World War I 124, 132-133
World War II 136-137, 149
Wrapper **62**, 63

Yataghan bayonet 127, **127**

159

SOME OTHER TITLES IN THIS SERIES

Natural History

The Animal Kingdom
Animals of Australia & New Zealand
Animals of Southern Asia
Bird Behaviour
Birds of Prey

Evolution of Life
Fishes of the World
Fossil Man
A Guide to the Seashore

Gardening

Chrysanthemums

Garden Flowers

Popular Science

Astronomy
Atomic Energy
Computers at Work

The Earth
Electricity
Electronics

Arts

Architecture

Jewellery

General Information

Coins and Medals
Flags
Guns

Military Uniforms
Rockets and Missiles

Domestic Animals & Pets

Budgerigars
Cats

Dog Care
Dogs

Domestic Science

Flower Arranging

History & Mythology

Archaeology
Discovery of
   Africa
   Australia
   Japan

Discovery of
   North America
   South America
   The American West